Excel

ADVANCED SKILLS

ENGLISH

YEAR 5

AGES 10–11

WRITING WORKBOOK

Get the Results You Want!

PASCAL PRESS

Laura Anderson

Reprinted 2017, 2018, 2020, 2021, 2023, 2024, 2026

ISBN 978 1 74125 405 1

Pascal Press
PO Box 250
Glebe NSW 2037
www.pascalpress.com.au

Publisher: Vivienne Joannou
Project editors: Mark Dixon and Leanne Poll
Edited by Leanne Howard
Series developer: Laura Anderson
Series consultant: Kristine Brown
Reviewed and answers checked by Glenda Walsh
Cover and page design by DiZign Pty Ltd
Typeset by Kim Webber
Printed by Vivar Printing/Green Giant Press

Contents

To the student

This book will help you with your writing tasks, in English and in other subjects.

There are ten units altogether, each focusing on a different type of text. Some texts are imaginative, such as narratives and poems. Others are factual, such as reports and explanations.

Each unit contains an introduction that explains the purpose of the text and its special features. There are also examples of students' first drafts. These are followed by practice exercises that aim to improve the draft. Some of the exercises focus on the structure of the text while others focus on its language features. There is one example of a student's final draft. Make sure you read it carefully and answer the questions beside each paragraph.

At the end of the unit is a text in which words, sentences or paragraphs are missing. You should try to fill in the missing sections, using the step-by-step improvement exercises to help you. In the final activity, you are given a list of topics and you have to choose one to write about.

Most of the activities can be written in this book, but you will have to use your own paper for the final writing activity. I suggest you buy a notebook or folder for this. If you are not sure how to write something, use the sample texts and the checklists to help you.

It is best to work through the book from Unit 1 to the end. This will help you build on skills you have already learnt. However, if you are learning about a particular type of text in school, you could do that unit in the book. For example, if you are learning about information reports, you could do Unit 5.

It is important that you have a dictionary and a thesaurus handy as you work through the book, and that you ask for help if you need it. There is also a word bank of useful vocabulary at the end of the book to help you with your writing.

I hope you enjoy reading the texts and doing the activities.

Good luck!

Laura Anderson

About this book

This book consists of ten units, each covering a different type of text. Each unit contains two samples of students' first drafts, followed by exercises designed to help the students improve their drafts. There is one example of a final draft, which models the text for students. Students are then asked to complete a partially constructed final draft, and finally to construct a text independently. These last two activities allow students to put the knowledge they have acquired into practice.

The units are organised as follows:

An introduction to the type of text

This page looks at the features of the text. There are also short exercises to help students identify the type of text or its features.

Student A: Writing the first draft

These two pages focus on the planning and writing of the first draft. There is a comprehensive checklist that enables students to identify the features that have or have not been included in the draft, as well as other short exercises.

A step-by-step improvement plan

This section contains four steps designed to help students improve the draft. Some of the steps focus on the structure of the text, while others focus on the language features.

Writing the final draft

The final draft is an example of a more advanced student's writing. It is accompanied by comments that point out the features of the text, as well as questions that ask students to identify some of the features.

Student B: Writing the first draft

The second half of the unit looks at another first draft, followed by a step-by-step improvement plan. Students are then asked to complete a partially constructed final draft.

Your turn

The final page of the unit contains a list of topics, from which students choose one to write about. There is a checklist to guide students in their writing. There is also a note directing students to a word bank at the back of the book where they can find useful vocabulary to help them with the writing task.

Word bank

At the end of the book is a word bank where students will find useful lists of words and phrases to help them complete their independent writing tasks.

Unit 1 Imaginative recounts—diary entries

Looking at recounts

A **recount** is generally an **informative** text. It tells about something that has already happened, in the order in which the events took place. Sometimes a recount might be about imaginary events based on things that really happened.

Examples of recounts include diary and journal entries, historical reports, letters, emails and postcards, newspaper reports and biographies or autobiographies.

The main **purpose** of a recount is to **inform** and to evaluate the importance of the events in some way. Recounts can also be entertaining.

A **recount** should have:

- an **orientation**, or introduction, that sets the scene. It tells the reader **who** was involved, **what** happened and **where**, **when** and sometimes **why** the events took place.
- a **sequence of events,** telling what happened in chronological order.
- a **conclusion**, which contains a **reorientation** to round off the sequence of events. It can also contain a personal comment about the events.

1 Which two texts below are LEAST likely to be the opening sentence of a **recount**? Tick (✓) the correct answers.

a We are having a wonderful time in Beijing!

b Choosy customers choose our shoes!

c A gas tank exploded in a factory in Ipswich early this morning.

d Across the stony ridges,
Across the rolling plain,
Young Harry Dale, the drover,
Comes riding home again.

e The most terrible thing happened to me this morning!

f Sir Edmund Barton, Australia's first prime minister, was born on January 18, 1849 in Glebe, Sydney.

2 Which of the texts below is a **recount**? Tick (✓) the correct answer.

a *Aboriginal people were the first human inhabitants of Australia. Before the arrival of the white settlers, there were about 300 000 Indigenous Australians scattered across the country.*

b *Bennelong, an Indigenous Australian, was captured in 1789. Three years later, he sailed with Governor Phillip to England, where he met King George III.*

Student A: Omar's draft

Omar's Year 5 class have been asked to imagine they are children living on the goldfields in the 1850s and to write **diary entries** recounting their time there. Omar is using the information on this poster to help him.

Life on the Goldfields

Food: Not much fresh food; ate mutton, dampers and drank tea

Dwellings: canvas tents, huts made from bark, wattle and daub huts

Schooling: Sometimes children taught by educated people, in tents or under trees

Daily activities: A hard life—children had to help carry water from creeks, gather firewood, wash clothes, cook and tend the horses. They also helped dig and look for gold.

Diggers using a cradle

Licence fees: Many diggers could not afford to pay the heavy licence fees

Collecting licence fees

Answer these questions using full sentences.

1. What type of homes did the diggers live in? ______________________________

____

2. What type of food did the diggers eat? ______________________________

____

3. What type of schooling did children on the goldfields receive? ______________________________

____

____

Writing the first draft

This is Omar's **first draft**. Read what he wrote and then answer the questions.

Victoria Goldfields, 16 July, 1853

This morning I woke up early. It was still dark outside.

First I had to bring in the firewood. Mother cooked breakfast. Then I went to the creek to get fresh water.

After breakfast I helped Pa at the diggings. I used the puddling pan. I didn't find any gold.

At ten o'clock I went to my lessons. Mr Murphy teaches some of the children to read, write and count. We meet in his tent for two hours every morning.

After that I went home for lunch. I collected firewood on the way.

I went back to the diggings with Pa. The men were complaining about the licence fees they had to pay to dig for gold. Then it got dark. We went home.

We had boiled mutton, damper and tea for dinner. Then I went to bed.

1. A good **recount** should contain the following features. Tick (✓) the ones that Omar has used.

   a an **orientation** that tells **who**, **what**, **when**, and **where** ☐

   b **events** told in the **order** in which they happened ☐

   c a **conclusion** containing a **personal comment** to round off the recount ☐

   d **time connectives** to link the **events** (e.g. *first, then* or *after that*) ☐

   e **conjunctions** to help the **writing flow** and **add detail** to sentences (e.g. *and, but* or *because*) ☐

   f **adjectives** that express **feelings** and **opinions** (e.g. *boring, exciting* or *exhausted*) ☐

   g interesting **information** and **detail** about the events ☐

   h **sentences** with **correct spelling** and **punctuation** ☐

2. One thing that Omar has done well in his draft is to link events with **time connectives**.

   a Underline all the time connectives in Omar's draft.

   b Find the following sentence in the draft and suggest a time connective that Omar could use to link it to the previous paragraph.

   ______________ I went back to the diggings with Pa.

Step-by-step improvement plan

Omar's **recount** does not contain enough interesting information and detail to keep his reader engaged. To improve it, he is going to do some practice exercises. Help him complete them.

Step 1: Start with a good orientation

The **orientation** needs to set the scene by telling **who**, **what**, **when** and **where**. It also needs to **capture** the **reader's attention** and make them want to read on.

Which of the **orientations** below would be a better way for Omar to start his recount?

A I woke up early this morning. It was still dark. I didn't want to leave my warm bed to go and fetch firewood. ☐

B I woke up at 5 o'clock this morning. It was still pitch dark outside and bitterly cold. I had to force myself to get out of my warm, snug bed to fetch in the firewood. ☐

C I woke up at 5 am. It was so dark I couldn't see a thing. I had to get up to go and fetch firewood for my mother. I didn't want to get up. ☐

Step 2: Link ideas with conjunctions

Conjunctions

- link words and phrases in sentences
- link simple sentences to make compound sentences
- help add detail to sentences
- make our writing flow
- include words like *and, but, or, so, yet, because, unless, until, when* and *while.*

Omar's writing does not flow because he has not used many conjunctions.

Use a **conjunction** from the list to complete each of these sentences. For some of the sentences there may be more than one possibility.

1. I brought in the firewood ____________ my mother could cook breakfast.
2. Father said I could use the puddling pan ____________ the cradle.
3. I used the puddling pan to look for gold, ____________ I didn't find anything.
4. ____________ we find gold, we will have to keep on living in our little canvas and bark hut.
5. I go to lessons with Mr Murphy ____________ Mother wants me to learn how to read and write.
6. I heard a kookaburra laughing in a nearby tree ____________ I was panning for gold.
7. We had to stop looking for gold ____________ it got dark.

Step 3: Add detail with adjectives

Adjectives give extra meaning to nouns. Some of them describe feelings.
For example: This is an **exciting** time.

Omar can add interest and colour to his writing by including some good feeling adjectives.

wonderful	angry	dissatisfied	despondent	dejected
unhappy	fantastic	hopeful	optimistic	furious
annoyed	excited	resentful	overjoyed	downcast

Choose three **adjectives** from the list to describe the following. Use each adjective only once.

1. how a digger would feel when he first arrived on the goldfields

2. how a digger would feel when he found gold

3. how a digger would feel after an unsuccessful day on the goldfields

4. how a child would feel about having to work so hard on the goldfields

5. how the diggers felt about the licence fees they had to pay

Step 4: End with a good conclusion

The **conclusion** is usually the last paragraph. It should include a **personal comment** to wrap up the recount.

Which **conclusion** contains a **personal comment**, making it a more effective way for Omar to wrap up his recount?

A After a dinner of mutton, damper and tea, I lit a candle and came to bed. And that is the end of another day without finding any gold. ☐

B Dinner was the usual mutton, damper and tea. Our neighbours joined us around the fire after dinner. We talked for a bit and then my mother said it was time for my sisters and me to go to bed. And that is the end of another day without finding any gold. ☐

C After dinner, which consisted of the usual mutton, damper and tea, I came to bed. It has been another long, hard day without finding any gold and I am exhausted. Once I've snuffed out the candle, I don't think it will take me long to fall asleep. ☐

Writing the final draft

This is Omar's **final draft**. Read the comments about his **recount** on the left, and do the tasks on the right.

Comments

A clear orientation tells **who**, **what**, **when** *and* **where**

Using **time connectives** *makes the writing flow and helps the reader make sense of the recount.*

Using **conjunctions** *makes the writing flow and helps add detail to sentences.*

Sequencing *events in the order in which they happened makes the recount easier to understand.*

Using **feeling adjectives** *adds interest and colour to the recount.*

The **conclusion** *contains a personal comment to round off the recount.*

Victoria Goldfields, 16 July, 1853

I woke up at 5 o'clock this morning. It was still pitch dark outside and bitterly cold. I had to force myself to get out of my warm, snug bed to fetch in the firewood so Mother could make breakfast.

After breakfast I went to the creek to get fresh water. I thought my hands were going to turn into ice blocks! I couldn't help comparing the life we'd left in Melbourne with the life we lead now. Life on the goldfields is so harsh! But Pa assures us that we will soon be rich.

When it got light I went with Pa to the diggings. He asked me if I wanted to use the puddling pan or the cradle. Today I chose the puddling pan, but I didn't find any gold.

At ten o'clock it was time for my lessons with Mr Murphy. Mother makes me go for two hours every day because she wants me to learn how to read, write and count.

After lunch I went back to the diggings with Pa. The men were complaining about the heavy licence fees they have to pay to dig for gold. Some of them were really angry! I fear there might be an uprising soon.

We packed up our tools as the last light of the day disappeared. We were a dejected bunch. We had worked hard all day but had dug up only worthless clay and gravel.

After dinner, which consisted of the usual mutton, damper and tea, I came to bed. It has been another long, hard day without finding any gold and I am exhausted. Once I've snuffed out the candle, I don't think it will take me long to fall asleep.

Tasks

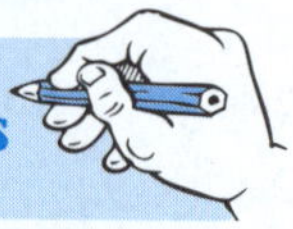

1. **Underline** the **conjunction** that links the idea of fetching firewood with Mother making breakfast.
2. **Underline** the **adjective** that means the opposite of *easy*.
3. **Underline** the **conjunction** that joins two sentences.
4. **Circle** the **conjunction** that introduces the reason for doing something.
5. **Circle** the **adjective** that describes how the men were feeling.
6. **Circle** the **adjective** that describes how the diggers felt when they packed up for the day.
7. **Underline** the **adjective** that describes how the writer was feeling at the end of the day.

Student B: Emily's draft

Emily is going to write about life on the goldfields from a young girl's point of view. She is using a different poster to help her.

LIFE ON THE GOLDFIELDS

Immigration: In the 1850s many people from around the world came to Australia in search of gold.

Journeying to Australia: The voyage from Europe took approximately five months on sailing ships like the *Sir Charles Napier*.

The sailing ship, *Sir Charles Napier*

Conditions on the goldfields: Very cold in winter and very hot in summer, smelly from the garbage lying around, water often polluted

Clothing: Girls wore pinafores over their long dresses, capes in winter, pantalettes to cover their legs, day-caps, and ribbons and silks if they were wealthy

Chores: Girls had to fetch and carry water, help wash the dishes and clothes, gather firewood, iron, knit and sew. Sometimes they helped pan for gold.

A family on the goldfields in the 1850s

Answer these questions using full sentences.

1. What type of weather did the diggers experience on the goldfields?

____

____

2. What made conditions on the goldfields unhygienic?

____

____

3. What did girls wear to protect their dresses?

____

____

4. How are girls' clothes today different from the clothes they wore in the 1850s?

____

____

Writing the first draft

This is Emily's **first draft**. Read it and then answer the questions.

Victoria, 14 May, 1855

Last week we arrived in Ballarat.

We came to Australia on the *Sir Charles Napier*. We disembarked in Melbourne. The journey took five months.

We had to buy a cart and horses to take us to the goldfields. Now we are at the goldfields.

The place smells. We have to get our water from the creek. The water is polluted. Mama says we must boil it before we drink it.

We are living in a canvas and bark hut. Papa says we're going to strike it rich. Then he'll order a prefabricated house for us from England.

I have lots of chores to do. I mainly fetch and carry water. I gather firewood. I also help to wash the dishes and clothes. Mama is teaching me how to knit and sew.

I made a friend the other day. Her name is Mary. She also comes from England.

1. Tick (✓) the correct answers. Which of these things has Emily remembered to include in her draft?

   - **a** a clear **orientation** that tells **who**, **what**, **when** and **where** ☐
   - **b** **events** told in the **order** in which they happened ☐
   - **c** a **conclusion** that contains a **personal comment** to round off the recount ☐
   - **d** **conjunctions** to **add detail** to sentences and make the **writing flow** ☐
   - **e** **adjectives** that express **feelings** and **opinions** ☐
   - **f** interesting **information** and **detail** about events ☐
   - **g** **sentences** with **correct spelling** and **punctuation** ☐

2. Read Emily's draft again and then rearrange these events by numbering them in the **order** in which they happened.

   - **a** found somewhere to live ☐
   - **b** made a friend ☐
   - **c** left England ☐
   - **d** arrived in Ballarat ☐
   - **e** arrived in Melbourne ☐

Step-by-step improvement plan

Emily also needs to improve her **recount** by adding more interesting information and detail, so like Omar, she is going to do some practice exercises. Can you help her?

Step 1: Start with a good orientation

Emily's orientation is not interesting enough to capture the reader's attention.

1. Which of these **opening paragraphs** is more likely to do so?

A. We left England almost six months ago. It took us five months to reach Australia. We came on a ship. The ship's name was the *Sir Charles Napier*. We landed in Melbourne. We had come in search of gold. ☐

B. When Papa said we were going to sail across the ocean to a place called Australia, I was very excited. It sounded like a big adventure. But I soon realised that being stuck on a ship for five months is no adventure at all. ☐

2. Now write your own **orientation** for Emily's recount.

____

____

____

____

Step 2: Link ideas with conjunctions

1. Emily is going to use some **conjunctions** to link her ideas. This will make her writing flow more smoothly and it will help add detail to her sentences. Complete each sentence with an ending from the box.

Mama says we must boil it before we drink it
the track was rough and bumpy
first we had to buy a cart and horses

a. Papa was keen to set out for the goldfields, but ____________________

____

b. It took us a long time to travel from Melbourne to Ballarat because __________

____

c. The water in the creek is dirty, so __________________________

____

2 Now write your own endings for these sentences.

a Mama says she won't be happy here until ______________________________

____

b Papa says he'll order a prefabricated house from England when ______________

____

c The birds in Australia are very beautiful, although ______________________

____

Step 3: Add detail with adjectives

Which **adjectives** from the box might Emily use to express the writer's feelings about the following? For example: she might feel *anxious* about leaving England to go to a strange land. Write down three adjectives below each heading.

1 The thought of leaving England to go to Australia	2 The journey from Melbourne to the goldfields	3 The goldfields

surprised	fascinated	anxious	curious	shocked
excited	nervous	confused	inquisitive	

Step 4: End with a good conclusion

Emily's conclusion is not effective because it does not round off her recount with a personal comment.

1 Which of these **conclusions** contains a **personal comment**?

A The houses in our village in England were built of stone and brick. There aren't really any proper houses on the goldfields. It rained a lot in England, but here there is more sunshine. The plants and animals are also different. ☐

B I like Australia because it is warmer and sunnier than England, but I miss my friends and family, especially my grandparents. Mama says that my grandparents might come to Australia when we have a proper house. That would make me very happy! ☐

2 Write a **personal comment** for the **conclusion** that does not have one.

____

____

Writing the final draft

Emily has started writing the **final draft** of her **recount**. Help her complete it by filling in the missing sections, and then look in the answers section to compare what you have written with what Emily wrote.

Hint! Look at the poster and practice exercises for ideas.

Victoria, 14 May, 1855

When Papa said we were going to sail across the ocean to a place called Australia, I was very excited. It sounded like a big adventure. But I soon realised that being stuck on a ship for five months is no adventure at all.

I was relieved when our ship, the *Sir Charles Napier*, finally docked in Melbourne. And that wasn't even the end of our journey! We still had to get to Ballarat.

The first thing Papa did in Melbourne was to buy a cart and horses. Then we set off for the goldfields! **(Tell about the journey to the goldfields, what it was like and what the writer and her family saw along the way.)**

....

....

....

....

....

We have been on the Ballarat goldfields for a week now. It isn't anything like I imagined it would be. I thought I would see lots of rich folk living in large houses and riding about in fine carriages, but most of the people here are very poor. **(Tell about the crowded and unhygienic conditions on the goldfields.)**

....

....

....

We live in a canvas and bark hut. Papa says he'll order a prefabricated house from England when we strike it rich. Mama says she won't be happy here until she has a decent house to live in. **(Tell how the writer felt about living in a hut.)**

....

....

....

I have lots of chores to do—more than I had in England. I mainly fetch and carry water and gather firewood. I also help wash the dishes and clothes, and Mama is teaching me how to knit and sew.

I made a friend the other day. Her name is Mary. She also comes from England. I am only allowed to go out and play with her if I have finished my chores. (Write your own conclusion, or choose one from the practice exercises.)

....

....

....

Your turn

Write a **recount** of one to two pages on one of the following. Use your own paper for this activity.

Writing Checklist Make sure your recount includes: ✓

- an **orientation** that sets the scene. ☐
- a **series of events**, told in the order in which they happened. ☐
- a **conclusion** that contains a **personal comment**. ☐
- **time connectives** to link events. ☐
- **conjunctions** to make your writing flow. ☐
- **adjectives** that express feelings and opinions. ☐
- interesting **information** and **detail**. ☐

Tip Use **Omar's final draft** on page 6 and **Emily's final draft** on page 11 to help you write your recount.

Go to WORD BANK page 134 for useful vocabulary

1. Imagine you are a 19th century girl or boy on one of the Australian goldfields. Write an imaginative recount telling about a day, a week or a few months in your life. Use Omar and Emily's recounts as models.
2. Ask your grandparents or an elderly relative or friend what life was like when they were your age. Where did they live? What did they do for fun? What did they learn about at school? What kind of clothes were fashionable? What kind of music did they listen to? Pretend you are a girl or boy living at that time and write an imaginative recount telling about a day or week in your life.

3. Pretend you are one of the students in this photograph from the 19th century. Write an imaginative recount telling about your school day.
4. Imagine what life might be like 100 years from now. Perhaps people will have robots to do chores around the house. They might travel around in flying cars, and classrooms could be virtual environments where students learn by being part of the action. Think of some other ways in which life could be different in the future, and then write an imaginative recount telling about a day in the life of a girl or boy from that time.

Unit 2 Descriptions—places

Looking at descriptions

A **description** can be **imaginative** or **informative**. Its aim is to give the reader a clear picture of a person, place or thing, often by involving the five senses.

A description is usually part of another text, so its **purpose** depends on its context. In a narrative, its main purpose is to **help tell the story**, while in a report or explanation, its purpose is generally to **inform**.

Sometimes, however, a description can be a text on its own. In this case, it should have:

- an interesting **introduction** that captures the reader's attention and tells **what** the description is about.
- a **series of paragraphs** that **describe** the subject.
- a **conclusion** that includes a **final comment** or **thought** about the person, place or thing.

Descriptions of people, places or things can form part of a:

- narrative.
- newspaper report.
- diary or journal entry.
- textbook.
- letter or email.
- magazine or website article.
- poem.
- advertisement.
- recount.

1 In which type of text are you most likely to find these **descriptions**? Write your answers in the spaces.

a Cinderella was a beautiful girl with long, blonde hair that shimmered with golden lights.

____

b Each creamy ice-cream bar is smothered in a thick layer of mouth-watering chocolate.

____

c I stood upon our western shore
And heard the ocean's billows roar.

____

2 Which text below is a **description** of a house? Tick (✓) the correct answer.

A We arrived at the big house late at night. We knocked on the front door, hoping that someone would answer it. Finally we heard muffled footsteps coming down the hall. ☐

B The house is a rectangular shape. It is painted white and has a steep slate roof. There is a brass knocker beside the beautifully carved front door. ☐

Student A: Hannah's draft

Hannah's Year 5 class have been asked to describe their favourite place. They have to involve all five senses in their **description**.

Hannah is going to write about the beach near her house.

Before she gets started, she imagines herself sitting on the beach and writes down all the things she can see, hear, touch or feel, smell and taste.

sand	ocean	umbrellas	people	yacht
people	children	chairs	lifeguards	food
sunscreen	sun	surfers	sky	seagulls
towel	salt	ship	water	waves

1 Sort Hannah's words into the correct categories and write them in the bubbles below. Some words, like *waves*, might belong to two or more categories.

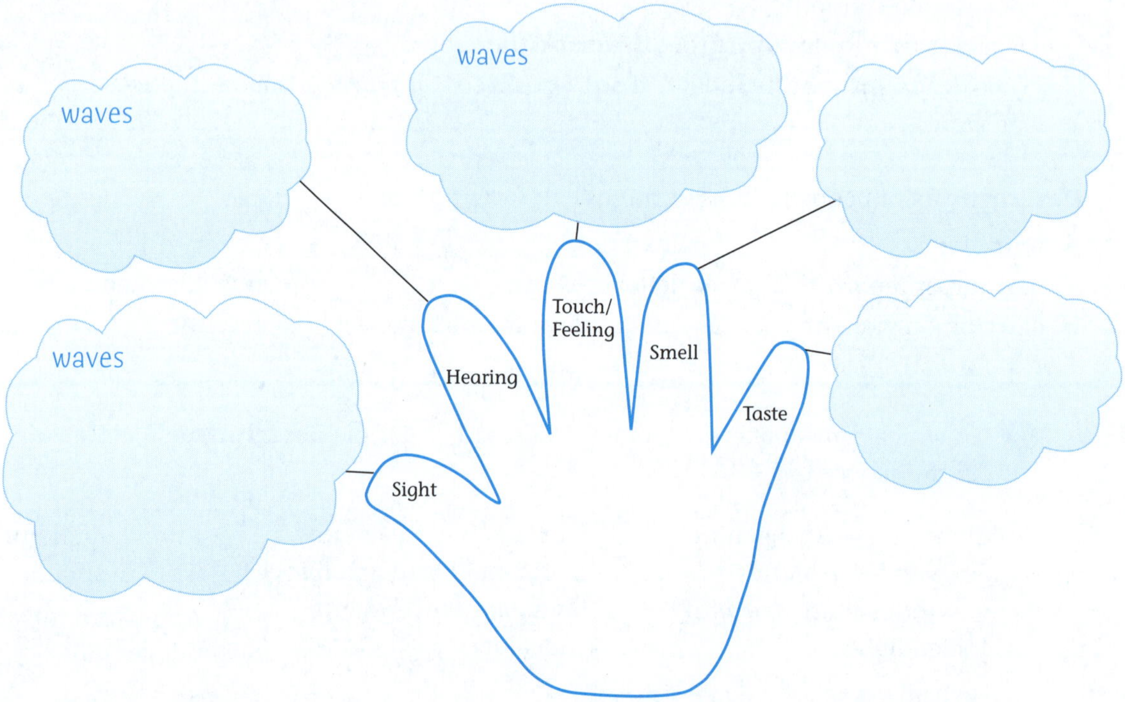

2 Think of more things that Hannah might see, hear, feel, smell, touch or taste at the beach and write them below.

Writing the first draft

This is Hannah's **first draft**. Read what she wrote and then answer the questions.

My Favourite Place

My favourite place is the beach near my house.

There are lots of interesting things to see at the beach. I like to sit on the sand and watch the people swimming in the water and the surfers riding the waves. Some people just sit on towels or chairs under beach umbrellas, and others play ball games.

I like listening to the sound of the waves and the children shouting to each other. Sometimes the lifeguards have to tell people to swim between the beacons.

I love to feel the sun on my back and the sand beneath my feet. I love the feel of the water around my legs.

I like the smell of the sea. It mixes with the smell of sunscreen and food from the nearby restaurants. After I've been swimming, I can even taste the salt on my lips.

The beach is my favourite place.

1. A good **description** should contain the following features. Tick the ones that Hannah has used.
   - a an **introduction** that captures the **reader's attention** ☐
   - b a series of **paragraphs** that **describe** the person, place or thing ☐
   - c a strong **conclusion** that includes a final **comment** or **thought** about the person, place or thing ☐
   - d **adjectives** that **describe** what people and things **look**, **sound**, **feel**, **smell** and **taste** like (e.g. **loud** *shouts*, **salty** *taste*) ☐
   - e **present-tense verbs** (e.g. *is*, *are* or *like*) ☐
   - f **noun groups** that include **interesting detail** (e.g. *the salty smell of the sea*) ☐
   - g **sentences** with **correct punctuation** and **spelling** ☐

2. Hannah has remembered to use **present-tense** verbs throughout her description. Underline the present-tense verbs in these sentences from the draft.
   - a My favourite place is the beach near my house.
   - b Some people just sit on towels or chairs under beach umbrellas, and others play ball games.
   - c I love the feel of the water around my legs.
   - d I like the smell of the sea.

Step-by-step improvement plan

Hannah clearly has some work to do to turn her draft into an interesting **description**. She is going to do some practice exercises to find ideas on how to improve it. Help her complete them.

Step 1: Start with an interesting introduction

The **introduction** is the opening paragraph. To **capture** the **reader's attention** and make them want to read on, the introduction must be interesting.

Hannah has jotted down some sentences to use in her introduction. Put them together to make an interesting **opening paragraph**.

I love the feel of the warm sun on my back.

I love the crunch of sand beneath my feet.

I get to experience these things at my favourite place– the beach near my house.

There are many things I love about the beach.

I love to watch the waves curling and crashing onto the shore.

____

____

____

____

____

Step 2: Paint a picture with adjectives

In Unit 1 you learnt that adjectives add information to nouns. By using interesting **adjectives** in her description, Hannah will give her reader a clearer picture of what people and things **look**, **sound**, **feel**, **smell** or **taste** like.

Complete the following sentences with **adjectives** from the box. Use each adjective once.

happy	suntanned	little	tall	bare
salty	soft	cold	delicious	sweet
creamy	spongy	warm	wet	

1. The sand feels ____________ and ____________ beneath my feet.
2. The ____________ smell of the sea mingles with the ____________ smell of sunscreen.
3. I shiver as the ____________ water creeps up my ____________ legs.
4. I hear the ____________ voices of ____________ children at play.
5. My ice-cream tastes ____________ and ____________.

Step 3: Add detail with noun groups

Noun groups are groups of words that are built around **nouns**. They tell who or what is involved in the sentence. They are a way of **adding detail** to sentences. For example, *my colourful* ***umbrella*** *with pink ribbons on top; my beach* ***umbrella*** *that I bought last week.*

1 Find an ending in the box to complete each of the **noun groups** below.

of a ship on the horizon	from nearby restaurants
topped with foamy white crests	squabbling over a chip
that feels like sugar beneath my feet	

a the white sand ______________________

b the blue-green waves ______________________

c two seagulls ______________________

d the faint outline ______________________

e delicious smells ______________________

Step 4: End with a strong conclusion

The **conclusion** is the final paragraph. It should contain a **comment** or **thought** about the topic to round off the description.

1 Which of these paragraphs contains a final comment or thought about the beach and would make a better **conclusion** for Hannah's description?

A I love going to the beach. There are lots of interesting things to see and do there. I also like the sound and smell of the sea. ☐

B When the sun begins to sink in the west, people start to pack up and leave. The waves take no notice. They continue to roll onto the beach, as they always have. ☐

2 Write a different **conclusion** for Hannah's description. Remember to include a final comment about the beach.

____

____

____

____

____

Writing the final draft

This is Hannah's **final draft**. Read the comments about her **description** on the left, and do the tasks on the right.

Comments

An interesting **introduction** *captures the reader's attention.*

Using **noun groups** *that contain interesting adjectives makes it easier for the reader to visualise what is being described.*

Using **descriptive verbs** *gives a clearer picture of the action and makes the writing more interesting to read.*

The **conclusion** *wraps up the description with a final comment about the beach.*

My favourite place

There are many things I love about the beach. I love the feel of the warm sun on my back. I love the crunch of sand beneath my feet. I love to watch the waves rolling onto the shore. I get to experience these things at my favourite place—the beach near my house.

After planting my umbrella in the soft sand and plastering sunscreen on my face and body, I settle down to enjoy the sights and sounds around me.

I am fascinated by the way the white-crested waves rise, curl and then crash onto the beach, spilling their foam across the sand. Sometimes I notice the faint outline of a ship on the horizon, or the white sails of a yacht bobbing up and down in the distance.

By late morning the beach is dotted with colourful beach umbrellas. Some of the people lie on their towels, soaking up the sun, while others frolic in the waves or play in the sand. The suntanned lifeguards, perched on their tall towers, keep a watchful eye on everyone.

I hear the happy shouts of little children as they shovel sand into plastic buckets. Some of them race about, spraying sand on sunbathers' legs. Usually there are seagulls nearby, squawking loudly as they squabble over scraps of food.

When I get too hot, I walk down to the water. The sharp smell of salt fills my nostrils and the cold water stings my bare legs.

As lunchtime approaches, delicious smells from nearby restaurants fill the air. They mingle with the salty smell of the sea and the sweet smell of sunscreen. Small grains of sand stick to my tongue as I chew on my chicken and salad sandwich.

When the sun begins to sink in the west, people start to pack up and leave. The waves take no notice. They continue to roll onto the beach, as they always have.

Tasks

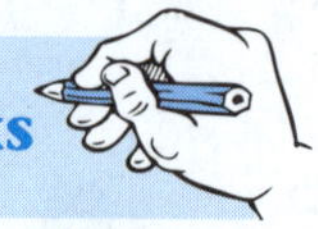

1. **Underline** the **noun group** that is built around the word 'place'.
2. **Circle** the **adjective** that describes the feel of the sand.
3. **Underline** the **adjective** that describes the appearance of the waves.
4. **Underline** the **noun groups** that are built around the words 'towers' and 'eye'.
5. **Circle** the **adjective** that describes the sound the children make.
6. **Underline** the **noun group** that is built around the word 'legs'.
7. **Underline** the **noun group** that is built around the word 'smells'.
8. **Highlight** the **final comment** about the beach.

Student B: Jose's draft

Jose's favourite place is his backyard, where he can let his imagination run wild.

Before writing his **description**, Jose makes a list of all the things in his backyard that he experiences with his five senses.

1. Place the words under the correct image, remembering that some things can be experienced with more than one sense.

tree	shovel	kennel	lawnmower
branches	barbecue	father	caterpillars
ladder	roses	vegetable patch	birds
tree house	deck	tomatoes	leaves
pathway	dog	lemons	grass

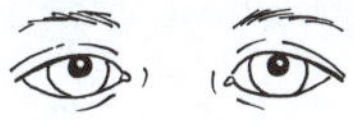		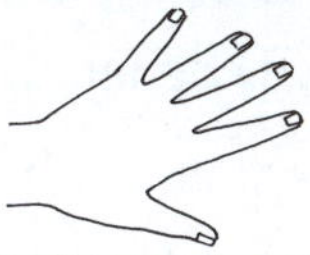		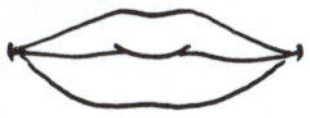

2. Think of more things that Jose might see, hear, feel, smell or taste in his backyard and add them to the list.

Writing the first draft

This is Jose's **first draft**. Read it and then answer the questions.

My Favourite Place

My favourite place is my backyard. That's where I let my imagination run wild.

My tree house is my secret hideout. I like to imagine I am watching over my kingdom from up there. Sometimes I see insects like caterpillars. They wriggle across the branches. Birds also like to sit in the tree.

A gravel pathway leads from the deck behind the house to the shed. We like to have barbecues on the deck. Inside the shed are the garden tools and lawnmower.

On one side of the pathway is a rose garden, a vegetable patch and a lemon tree. On the other side is grass. My dog's kennel is next to the shed.

The best vegetables in the vegetable patch are the tomatoes. They taste good. There are also lots of lemons on the lemon tree. They have a fresh smell.

I like to watch my dad when he mows the lawn. My dog doesn't like the sound of the lawnmower. She runs away when she hears it.

My backyard is my favourite place.

1. Which of these features has Jose remembered to use in his draft?
   - a an **introduction** that **captures** the **reader's attention** ☐
   - b a series of **paragraphs** that **describe** his backyard ☐
   - c a **conclusion** that includes a **final thought** about his backyard ☐
   - d **adjectives** that **describe** how things **look**, **sound**, **feel**, **smell** and **taste** ☐
   - e **present-tense verbs** ☐
   - f **noun groups** that include interesting **adjectives** ☐
   - g **sentences** with the correct **spelling** and **punctuation** ☐

2. Jose has remembered to use **present-tense verbs** throughout his draft. Which verb tells what
   - a the caterpillars do? ______________________
   - b the birds do? ______________________
   - c Dad does? ______________________
   - d the dog does? ______________________

Step-by-step improvement plan

Jose is also going to do some practice exercises to improve his draft. Help him complete them.

Step 1: Start with an interesting introduction

1 Which of these **opening paragraphs** would be more likely to capture the reader's attention?

A My favourite place is where I get to be a superhero. It's where I'm a pirate searching for treasure, or a famous explorer discovering unknown lands. It's the magical kingdom behind my house. It's my backyard. ☐

B My favourite place is my backyard. The reason it's my favourite place is because I can have fun there. I can create my own world there, so it can be whatever I want it to be. I also like to explore my backyard because it is full of interesting things. ☐

2 Write a different **introduction** for Jose's description. Remember that it must hook the reader in!

____

____

____

____

____

Step 2: Paint a picture with adjectives

Use interesting **adjectives** to describe the following nouns. The first one has been done for you.

Noun	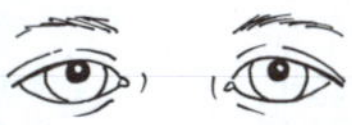		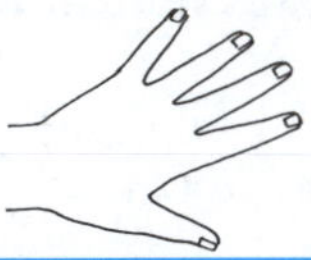		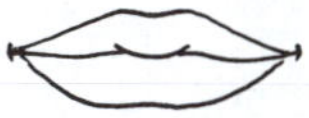
1 roses	beautiful		velvety	fragrant	
2 barbecue					
3 soil					
4 branches					
5 dog					
6 tree house					
7 lawnmower					

Step 3: Add detail with noun groups

Build interesting **noun groups** around the following words.

For example: kingdom the magical kingdom behind my house

1. shed ____
2. tree ____
3. caterpillars ____
4. birds ____
5. tomatoes ____
6. grass ____
7. lemons ____

Step 4: End with a strong conclusion

1. Rearrange the sentences on the notes to make a good **conclusion** for Jose's description. Remember that good conclusions often end with a **personal comment**.

a My backyard truly is a magical place! ☐

b I spend hours up there—watching fat green caterpillars wriggling along the branches and listening to the birds twittering or squawking around me. ☐

c The thing I like best about my backyard is my tree house. ☐

d It's where I let my imagination run wild. ☐

2. Now write a different **conclusion** for Jose's description. Don't forget to add a comment about his backyard!

____

____

____

____

____

____

____

____

____

Writing the final draft

Jose has started writing the **final draft** of his **description**. Complete it by filling in the missing sections, and then look in the answer section to compare what you have written with what Jose wrote.

Hint! Look at the practice exercises for ideas.

My favourite place

My favourite place is where I get to be a superhero. It's where I'm a pirate searching for treasure, or a famous explorer discovering unknown lands. It's the magical kingdom behind my house. It's my backyard.

In one corner is a large tree with spreading branches. A sturdy rope ladder leads up to a cosy tree house. I sometimes pretend this is my secret hideout from where I can keep watch over my kingdom.

Opposite the tree is the shed, where Dad keeps his tools. A gravel pathway runs from the wooden deck behind the house to the shed. I like listening to the crunch of Dad's gardening boots as he strides down the pathway. Sometimes I imagine he is a pirate coming to find my treasure!

The wooden deck is where we have our Sunday barbecues. **(Write about one of Jose's barbecues, remembering to describe the sounds, smells and tastes.)**

....

....

....

....

....

....

....

Next to the shed is our labrador's kennel. The only time she ever uses it is when Dad mows the grass. As soon as the mower roars into life, Sheba howls and takes refuge inside her little house.

On one side of the pathway is a rose garden, a vegetable patch and a lemon tree. **(Write about the roses, the tomatoes in the vegetable patch and the lemon tree, remembering to describe what they look, feel, smell or taste like.)**

....

....

(Write a good conclusion that includes a personal comment.)

Your turn

Write a **description** of one to two pages on one of the following. Use your own paper for this activity.

Writing Checklist Make sure your description has: ✓

- an **introduction** that captures the reader's attention. ☐
- a **series** of **paragraphs** that describe the place or subject you are writing about. ☐
- a **conclusion** that contains a **final comment** about the place you are describing. ☐
- **adjectives** that describe what people and things look, sound, feel, smell or taste like. ☐
- **noun groups** that contain interesting **adjectives**. ☐

Tip Use **Hannah's final draft** on page 18 and **Jose's final draft** on page 23 to help you write your description.

Go to WORD BANK page 134 for useful vocabulary

1. Write a description of your favourite place, such as the attic, your cubby house or your local park or reserve. Use Hannah and Jose's descriptions as models.
2. Find a picture of a place you would like to visit. Imagine you are there, experiencing it through your five senses of sight, hearing, touch, smell and taste.

Unit 3 Narratives

Looking at narratives

A **narrative** tells a story. Its main **purpose** is to **entertain**, but some narratives teach us more about the world and some may even inspire us to behave differently or to follow our dreams. Fables, for example, contain lessons about how we should or should not behave.

A **narrative** should have:

- an **orientation** that sets the scene by telling the reader **who**, **where**, **when** and **what**.
- a **complication** or **problem** that has to be **resolved**, usually by the main character.
- a **series of events** that result from the **complication**.
- a **resolution**, in which the problem is **solved**.

1 Which type or category of **narrative** do you enjoy writing about? Choose one from the list.

Adventure	☐	Folk tales	☐	Mystery	☐
Fables	☐	Historical	☐	Myths	☐
Fairy tales	☐	Horror	☐	Realistic	☐
Fantasy	☐	Humorous	☐	Science fiction	☐

2 Match the titles below with the type of **narrative** they are most likely to be.

a *The Tunnel in the Mountain* ______________

b *The Talking Hat* ______________

c *The Golden Egg* ______________

d *The Box* ______________

e *The Faraway Kingdom* ______________

f *The Missing Ring* ______________

g *The Haunted House* ______________

h *The Time Machine* ______________

i *How the Bear Lost Its Tail* ______________

j *1788* ______________

Perhaps you were undecided about some of the titles. For most of them there is more than one possibility.

3 Which of these texts is more likely to be part of a **narrative**?

A A rocket is a jet engine. It is used to blast a missile or other vehicle into space. ☐

B After what seemed like only a few minutes, they were soaring above the earth. ☐

Student A: Sarah's draft

Sarah's Year 5 class have to choose one of the **narrative** types to write about. Sarah is going to write a fairy tale about how the dragon got its fire.

Sarah's first step is to create a mind map so that she can organise her thoughts and ideas.

In the first two units you learnt that adjectives add colour and interest to writing.

Which **adjectives** might Sarah use to describe the following?

1. dragons ______________________________
2. mountains ______________________________
3. humans ______________________________
4. volcano ______________________________
5. lava ______________________________
6. fire ______________________________

Writing the first draft

This is Sarah's **first draft**. Read it and then answer the questions.

How the Dragon Got Its Fire

Long ago some dragons lived in the mountains. In those days they couldn't breathe fire. They ate humans.

One little dragon called Flamma didn't like the taste of humans. He wouldn't eat them. The other dragons teased him. He was very unhappy. He decided to run away. He knew if he went to the great volcano the other dragons wouldn't follow him. They were afraid of fire.

At first Flamma was scared of the smoke and fire coming from the volcano. He didn't know that the fire wouldn't burn him. Soon Flamma started to feel hungry. He ate some lava. It tasted good. He ate so much he started to hiccup. Fire came out of his nostrils. Soon he was breathing fire. He went back to the mountains, but the other dragons started teasing him again.

Flamma showed them how to breathe fire and he was a hero.

1 A good **narrative** should contain the following features. Tick (✓) the ones that Sarah has used.

- **a** a clear **orientation** that **sets the scene** ☐
- **b** an interesting **complication** ☐
- **c** a **series** of **events** divided into **paragraphs** ☐
- **d** a strong **resolution** that shows how the problem is solved and provides a satisfying **conclusion** to the story ☐
- **e** **descriptive verbs** (e.g. *roared, flashed* or *wept*) ☐
- **f** **past tense verbs** (e.g. *teased* or *decided*) ☐
- **g** **similes and metaphors** (e.g. *as sweet as syrup; ribbons of fire*) ☐
- **h** **dialogue** to make the characters come to life (e.g. *"Why are you so sad?"* she asked.) ☐
- **i** interesting **information** and **detail** about the events ☐
- **j** **sentences** with **correct spelling** and **punctuation** ☐

2 One thing Sarah has remembered to do is to use **past tense** verbs. Underline the past tense of these verbs in her draft.

a eat **b** go **c** are **d** is **e** come

Step-by-step improvement plan

At this stage, Sarah's **narrative** lacks interest and excitement. She is going to do some practice exercises to find ideas on how to improve it. Help her complete the exercises.

Step 1: Add interest with descriptive verbs

Verbs tell **what** happens and **when** it happens. Some verbs are more descriptive than others; (e.g. *stroll* is more descriptive than *walk* because it tells us exactly **how** the person is walking). Using **descriptive verbs** makes a narrative more interesting to read.

1 Replace the underlined verbs in these sentences with a more **descriptive verb** from the box.

gazed | perched | curled | flapped | spewing | flee | gobbled | swoop

a The dragons would fly ____________ down from the high mountains.

b Flamma was so unhappy he decided to go ____________ to the great volcano.

c Flamma moved ____________ his wings and rose up into the air.

d Flamma stood ____________ on the edge of the volcano.

e He looked ____________ at the fire and lava coming ____________ out of it.

f He ate ____________ so much lava that he started to hiccup.

g Each time he hiccupped, flames came ____________ out of his nostrils.

2 Write another descriptive verb in place of

a ate ____________ b looked ____________

Step 2: Add colour with similes and metaphors

Similes compare one thing to something else which is usually dissimilar, using the words *like* or *as*.

For example: Flamma's skin was **as** rough **as** sandpaper.
Flamma's skin was **like** sandpaper.

Metaphors compare one thing to something else by saying that it is that thing.
For example: The lava **was** a fiery snake winding its way down the mountain.

Similes and **metaphors** help the reader visualise the people, places and events. Like descriptive verbs, they add interest to the text.

1 Complete these sentences with a **simile** or **metaphor** from the box.

like little streams | like fireworks | like warm syrup | rivers of lava | a roaring giant

a Tears flowed down Flamma's cheeks ________________________ .

b Red sparks shot into the air ________________________ .

c The volcano was ________________________ waiting to swallow him!

d ________________________ flowed down the side of the mountain.

e The lava slid down his throat ________________________ .

2. Underline the phrase in brackets that is a metaphor.

   To Flamma's surprise, (little flames/ribbons of fire) shot out of his nostrils.

Step 3: Bring characters to life with dialogue

Dialogue is the actual words characters use in a text. If used properly, it can bring the characters to life, so it is another way of adding **interest** and **energy** to narratives.

Reminder! It is important that you punctuate dialogue correctly.

- Use **speech marks** (" ") around the actual words that a character speaks, **including** any punctuation.
- Use a **capital letter** when someone speaks for the first time, even if the first spoken word comes after a comma.
- Start a **new paragraph** when a new character starts speaking.
  For example: "Why are you unhappy, Flamma?" asked his mother.
  Flamma replied, "All the other dragons are teasing me."

Fill in the missing **speech marks** in these sentences.

1. Oh, Flamma, they howled, how can you call yourself a dragon when you won't eat humans?
2. Oh dear, sighed Flamma, what am I going to do?
3. So where have you been, Flamma? Frightening humans? they asked.
4. I'm so proud of you, Flamma, said his mother.
5. Don't be frightened, said Flamma, I'll show you all how to breathe fire.
6. We're so sorry we were mean to you said the dragons. Please forgive us.

Hint! Don't drown your narrative in dialogue! It is more effective if used sparingly.

Step 4: End with a strong resolution

The **resolution** is the final paragraph or two of the **narrative** in which the problem is solved. It should wrap the story up and provide a **satisfying ending**.

Which is the more effective ending?

A Flamma breathed out hard—"Whoosh!" Long, red ribbons of flame burst out of his nostrils. The other dragons drew back in fear, but Flamma told them not to be frightened. He explained how the great volcano had given him this wonderful gift and soon all the dragons who lived in the high mountains were breathing fire. Now they no longer teased Flamma. He was a hero! ☐

B Flamma didn't cry when the other dragons teased him because he knew they would be impressed that he could breathe fire. He couldn't wait to show them the fire coming out of his nostrils. At first they were scared, but then they all wanted to breathe fire. Flamma showed them how and they all lived happily ever after. ☐

Writing the final draft

This is Sarah's **final draft**. Read the comments about her **description** on the left, and do the tasks on the right.

Comments

A clear ***orientation*** *sets the scene.*

An interesting ***complication*** *draws the reader in.*

A bit of ***dialogue*** *adds energy to the text.*

Starting a new ***paragraph*** *each time a new idea is introduced makes the text easier to understand.*

Using a mixture of ***short and long sentences*** *adds interest to the text.*

Including interesting ***detail*** *makes it easier for the reader to visualise the events.*

An effective ***resolution*** *wraps the story up and provides a satisfying ending.*

How the Dragon Got Its Fire

Long ago, before dragons could breathe fire, they lived in the high mountains and ate humans.

But one little dragon was different from the others. He refused to eat humans. The other dragons teased him until the tears rolled down his cheeks like little streams.

"Oh, Flamma!" they howled. "How can you call yourself a dragon when you won't eat humans?"

Flamma was so miserable that he decided to run away. In those days dragons were afraid of fire, so Flamma knew that if he went to the great volcano, the other dragons wouldn't follow him.

Early the next morning Flamma set off, and it wasn't long before he was perching nervously on the edge of the crater. The volcano rumbled menacingly. Red-hot sparks rained down on him. Smoke crawled up his nostrils. Flamma was certain the volcano was going to roast him, but the fire and smoke didn't hurt him—it made him feel good!

Flamma looked at the rivers of bubbling lava flowing down the side of the volcano. They looked tasty! He bit off a chunk. It slid down his throat like warm syrup. He kept on eating the delicious lava until his tummy was almost bursting! Then he hiccupped. A little flame curled out of his nostril. He hiccupped again, and this time the flame was bigger. Flamma flew back to his home in the mountains. He couldn't wait to show the other dragons how he could breathe fire.

When he landed on the grassy area in front of the main cave, the other dragons gathered around him.

"So where have you been, Flamma? Frightening humans again?" they asked, and they burst out laughing.

"Whoosh!" said Flamma, as he breathed out hard. Long red ribbons of flame burst out of his nostrils. The other dragons drew back in fear, but Flamma told them not to be frightened. He explained how the great volcano had given him this wonderful gift and soon all the dragons who lived in the high mountains were breathing fire. Now they no longer teased Flamma. He was a hero!

Tasks

1. **Circle** the **simile**.
2. **Underline** the **actual** words the dragons use.
3. **Circle** the **descriptive verbs** in red and underline the **adjectives** in blue.
4. **Underline** the **metaphor**.
5. **Underline** the **dialogue**.
6. **Circle** the **sound word**.

Student B: Stuart's draft

Stuart, another Year 5 student, prefers writing adventure stories.
He has chosen the title *Washed Away* for his **narrative**. He is also using a mind map to organise his thoughts and ideas.

In Unit 2 you learnt that adjectives help paint a picture for readers.

Add to these lists of **adjectives** that Stuart could use when describing

1. the storm fierce, raging, ______________________________
2. how he felt when he was washed away frightened, scared, ______________________________
3. how he felt when he was rescued happy, relieved, ______________________________

Writing the first draft

This is Stuart's **first draft**. Read it and then answer the questions.

Washed Away

Ben, Chan and I went camping.

A storm woke us up in the early hours of the morning. The creek had flooded. I unzipped the tent. Ben and Chan made it to higher ground, but I didn't. The water swept me away.

The water was flowing very strongly. Suddenly I felt as if I was trapped in something. It was very dark. I couldn't see a thing. I was very frightened. I think I dozed off.

When I woke up it was getting light. I saw buildings. Then I heard voices. People came and saved me.

I had to go to hospital, but I only had scratches and bruises. Otherwise I was fine. It hasn't stopped me going camping.

1. Which of these features has Stuart remembered to include in his draft? Tick (✓) the correct answers.

   a a clear **orientation** that **sets the scene** ☐

   b an interesting **complication** ☐

   c a **series of events** divided into **paragraphs** ☐

   d a strong **resolution** that shows how the problem is **solved** and provides a satisfying **conclusion** to the story ☐

   e interesting **information** and **detail** about the events ☐

   f **sentences** with **correct spelling** and **punctuation** ☐

2. Which of these **language features** has Stuart used in his draft?

   a descriptive verbs ☐

   b similes and metaphors ☐

   c past tense ☐

   d dialogue ☐

Step-by-step improvement plan

At this stage, Stuart's **narrative** is rather dull. To find ideas on how to make it more interesting and exciting, he is also going to do some practice exercises. Help him complete them.

Step 1: Start with an interesting orientation

The **orientation** is the opening paragraph or two of a narrative. It should be interesting enough to capture the reader's attention and give them a clearer picture of **who**, **when**, **where** and **what**.

1 Which of these **orientations** works better?

A Ben, Chan and I had spent the day hiking through rough bush. Just as the sun was dipping below the horizon, we came to a shady spot next to a small creek. We decided it was a good place to set up camp. After a quick meal of canned soup and dry crackers, we flopped into our sleeping bags. We were asleep in no time. ☐

B My friends and I like hiking. Once we went hiking in the bush. We hiked all day. That night we put up our tent near a creek. The creek didn't have much water in it. We made something to eat and then we talked for a bit. We were very tired, so we rolled out our sleeping bags and climbed into them. ☐

2 Now write a different **orientation** for Stuart's narrative.

____

____

____

____

____

____

____

Step 2: Add interest with descriptive verbs

Stuart can make his narrative more interesting and exciting by using more **descriptive verbs**.

1 Complete each sentence with the most **descriptive verb** from the box.

get	flashing	scramble	bucketing	tossing	shining
hauled	grasped	rushing	brought	moving	slammed

a The rain was ____________ down.

b Lightning was ____________ all around us.

c Ben and Chan managed to ____________ to safety.

d The flood water ____________ into me and started ____________ me about.

e I stopped moving, but I could still hear the water ____________ past me.

f Strong hands ____________ my shoulders and ____________ me out of the water.

2 Write two or three **descriptive verbs** that can be used in place of the following.

a said ______________________

b looked ______________________

c ran ______________________

d pushed ______________________

Step 3: Add colour with similes and metaphors

1 Choose the **metaphor** that best describes the *force* of the water as it slammed into the narrator.

a a curtain of water ☐

b a wall of water ☐

c a fountain of water ☐

2 Which **simile** best describes how *helpless* the narrator felt in the water?

a The water tossed me about like a robot. ☐

b The water tossed me about like an action hero. ☐

c The water tossed me about like a rag doll. ☐

3 Choose the **simile** that best describes how *dark* it was that night.

a The darkness was as thick as a blanket. ☐

b The darkness was as thick as a scarf. ☐

c The darkness was as thick as a veil. ☐

4 Which **simile** best describes how *frightened* the narrator felt in the water?

Fear gripped my heart ____________ .

a like a paw ☐ b like a hand ☐ c like a claw ☐

5 Replace this overused **simile** with a more original one.

as quick as a wink

as quick as ____________

Step 4: Bring characters to life with dialogue

Which sentence in the following pairs suggests the urgency of the situation?

1

A "I think the creek is going to come down in flood and it might wash us away," I said when I heard the rain beating against the tent. ☐

B "Quickly!" I yelled, as I unzipped the tent. "We have to get to higher ground!" ☐

2

A "Over here!" someone shouted. "Hurry!" ☐

B "Can somebody please help me get this boy out of the river?" I heard a voice say. ☐

Writing the final draft

Stuart has started writing the **final draft** of his **narrative**. Help him complete it by filling in the missing sections, and then look in the answers section to compare what you have written with what Stuart wrote.

Hint! Look at Stuart's mind map and practice exercises for ideas.

Washed Away

Ben, Chan and I had spent the day hiking through rough bush. Just as the sun was dipping below the horizon, we came to a shady spot next to a small creek. We decided it was a good place to set up camp. After a quick meal of canned soup and dry crackers, we flopped into our sleeping bags. We were asleep in no time.

We were woken in the early hours of the morning by the sound of crashing thunder. Lightning was flashing all around us and the rain was bucketing down. We knew the creek could come down in flood at any moment. We had to get to higher ground.

Quickly we unzipped the front of the tent. Ben and Chan went ahead of me and managed to scramble to safety. I was too late. A wall of water slammed into me and started tossing me about like a rag doll.

After what seemed like hours, **(Tell how the narrator was washed downstream.)**

I must have dozed off, because when I opened my eyes, I could make out the outlines of buildings against the pale sky. I glanced down and saw that I had been saved by a tangle of branches and wood that had become stuck against a large rock, with me wedged in between. But I couldn't move. I was numb with cold and exhaustion.

Then I heard voices. **(Tell how the narrator was rescued.)**

I spent the next couple of days in hospital, but apart from a few scratches and bruises, I was fine.

I still go camping, but now I make sure I stay away from the banks of rivers and creeks!

Your turn

Write a **narrative** of one to two pages on one of the following. Use your own paper for this activity.

Writing Checklist Make sure your narrative contains: ✓

- a **title**. ☐
- an **orientation** that captures the reader's attention and sets the scene by telling **who**, **what**, **where** and **when**. ☐
- an interesting **complication** or problem. ☐
- a **series of events** divided into paragraphs. ☐
- a **resolution** in which the problem is resolved. ☐
- **descriptive verbs**, **figurative language** and **some dialogue**. ☐
- interesting **information** and **detail** about the events. ☐

Tip Use **Sarah's final draft** on page 30 and **Stuart's final draft** on page 35 to help you write your narrative.

Go to WORD BANK pages 134–135 for useful vocabulary

1. Jodie found the bracelet on her way home from school. It was lying beside the pathway, half hidden by the grass that grew longer where it met the concrete, like the stubble on an old man's chin. Without thinking, Jodie picked up the bracelet and slipped it onto her wrist.

   Suddenly …

   Continue the narrative.

2. Write a narrative that ends with the following paragraph.

   The food finally arrived and the party went ahead. Everyone agreed afterwards that they'd had a great time, even though the day hadn't gone as planned!

3. Choose the type of narrative you most like writing about from the list at the beginning of the unit. Write an interesting story.

Unit 4 Expositions—speeches

Looking at expositions

An **exposition** is an **argument**. It states a particular **position** or **point of view** and gives evidence to support it. Its main **purpose** is to **persuade** people that this particular point of view is the right one.

An **exposition** can take many forms—it might be in:

- a speech.
- a letter to a newspaper or magazine.
- an email to an organisation or individual.
- an article in a brochure, magazine or newspaper.
- a blog.

In this unit we will be looking at expositions in speeches.

When making a **speech**, it is important for the speaker to **engage** with the audience by **talking directly** to them. Some ways a speaker can do this is by using **personal pronouns** such as *you*, *we* and *us*, and by **asking questions** to make the audience think about the issue.

An **exposition** should have:

- an **opening paragraph** that states the **position** or **point of view**.
- **arguments** that give reasons for the point of view.
- **evidence** to support the arguments.
- a **conclusion** that **repeats** the point of view and **refers back** to the arguments.

1 Which of the following sentences expresses a **point of view**?

a There are many high-rise buildings in our neighbourhood. ☐

b I believe there are too many high-rise buildings in our neighbourhood. ☐

2 In a speech, which sentence is more likely to capture an audience's **attention**?

a Lots of the food in the canteen is unhealthy. ☐

b Are you aware that lots of the food in the canteen is unhealthy? ☐

Student A: Angelo's draft

The Year 5s have raised $1000 to improve facilities at the school.
Angelo's class have been asked what they think the money should be spent on and to present their arguments as **speeches**.

Angelo believes the money should be spent on improving the school grounds by planting more trees.

First, he did some research to make sure he had strong arguments and evidence to support his position. He made these rough notes of his findings.

clean the air—good for our health—attract wildlife—help conserve wildlife—change carbon dioxide into oxygen—cool the atmosphere—lungs of the earth—provide shade—provide food for birds and insects—release moisture into atmosphere—protect us from sun's rays—many birds, insects, small mammals make homes in trees—prevent sunburn—keep us cool

Fill in the evidence that Angelo could use to support these arguments.

Argument	Supporting evidence
1 Good for our health	
2 Good for the environment	
3 Keep us cool	

Writing the first draft

This is Angelo's **first draft**. Read it and then answer the questions.

> I believe we should spend the money on more trees for the school grounds. These are my reasons.
>
> Trees are good for our health. They change carbon dioxide into oxygen. We need oxygen to breathe. Trees are the lungs of the earth and they stop the sun from burning our skins.
>
> Trees are good for the environment. They attract and help conserve wildlife. Lots of birds, insects and mammals live in trees. They get their food from trees. Trees also clean the air.
>
> Trees keep us cool. They give us shade and they cool the atmosphere.
>
> That's why I think we need to spend the money on more trees for the school grounds.

1 A good **exposition** should contain the following features. Tick (✓) the ones that Angelo has used.

- **a** an **opening paragraph** that contains the **statement of position** or **point of view**, plus some background information ☐
- **b** a series of **arguments** that give **reasons** for the point of view ☐
- **c** strong, detailed **evidence** to **support** the **arguments** ☐
- **d** a **conclusion** that **repeats** the point of view and **refers back** to the arguments ☐
- **e** **thinking** and **feeling verbs** (e.g. *believe, know*) ☐
- **f** **modal verbs** and **adverbs** (e.g. *will, must*) ☐
- **g** **present-tense verbs** (e.g. *are, clean*) ☐
- **h** **connectives** to link **arguments** (e.g. *Firstly, In addition*) ☐
- **i** **sentences** with **correct spelling** and **punctuation** ☐

2 Angelo has remembered to use some thinking and feeling verbs in his draft. Find them in the text and underline them.

Step-by-step improvement plan

Angelo's arguments are not strong enough to persuade an audience to his point of view. He is going to do some practice exercises to try and make his **speech** more convincing. Help him complete them.

Step 1: Start with a good introduction

The **introduction** is the opening statement of the speech. It should include the speaker's **point of view**, but it should also be interesting enough to **capture** the **audience's attention** and make them want to listen.

Angelo's introduction is not interesting enough to capture his audience's attention.

1. Which of these **opening paragraphs** would be a better way for Angelo to start his speech?

A. Imagine it is a really hot day. Where would you rather sit—on a bench in the blazing sun, or on the grass beneath a shady tree? I am sure you would all choose the shady tree. This is one reason I think we should spend the $1000 on trees for the school grounds, but there are others too. ☐

B. Trees are important. They will make our school grounds more beautiful. We should use the $1000 to buy trees. We can plant them all around the school. There are also other reasons why we should spend the money on trees. ☐

2. Highlight the **question** in one of the paragraphs.

Step 2: Link ideas with connectives

Connectives are words and phrases that link paragraphs, sentences and parts of sentences in a text. They can be

- **adverbs** (e.g. *firstly, also, finally*).
- **adverbial phrases** (e.g. *in the first place, in addition*).
- **conjunctions** (e.g. *and, but, so, or, because, although*).

1. Complete this version of Angelo's draft with **connectives** from the box. Use each connective once.

also	firstly	for example	in addition	and	therefore	because	secondly

I believe we should spend the money on more trees for the school grounds. These are my reasons.

____________, trees are good for our health _______ they clean the air by absorbing carbon dioxide ____________ turning it into oxygen. ____________, trees attract birds, insects and small mammals. These animals play an important role in the environment. Birds, ____________, help with pest control by eating unwelcome visitors such as mosquitoes. ____________, trees protect us from the harsh rays of the sun. They ____________ cool the atmosphere by releasing moisture into the air. In the hot summer months, ____________, more trees in the school grounds will protect us from the sun and keep us cool.

Step 3: Show certainty with modal verbs and adverbs

Modal verbs are auxiliary verbs. We use them to show how **certain** we are about something. This is called **modality**.

Auxiliary verbs that show **certainty** have **high modality**.

For example: must, must not, will, will not, should, should not.

Auxiliary verbs that show **uncertainty** have **low modality**.

For example: might, might not, could, could not, may, may not

Adverbs can also have **modality**. Adverbs with high modality include *definitely, certainly, surely, always* and *never*. Adverbs with low modality include *perhaps, maybe, usually, probably* and *sometimes*.

Rank the sentences below from **most certain** (1) to **least certain** (3). Write the numbers in the boxes.

1. a Planting trees might add beauty and character to the school grounds. ☐
   b Planting trees will add beauty and character to the school grounds. ☐
   c Planting trees should add beauty and character to the school grounds. ☐

2. a Perhaps we could plant some trees near the basketball court. ☐
   b We could probably plant some trees near the basketball court. ☐
   c We should definitely plant some trees near the basketball court. ☐

Step 4: End with a strong conclusion

The **conclusion** is the final statement the speaker makes. It is their last chance to impress the audience, so it should be as effective as possible.

1. Which **conclusion** is more likely to impress Angelo's audience?

A I hope you will listen to my arguments and spend the money on trees for the school grounds. We really need them. They help us and the insects, birds and other animals. Please spend the money on buying trees for the school grounds. ☐

B I hope my arguments have persuaded you that the $1000 should be spent on trees for the school grounds. Not only will we be adding beauty and character to our school, but we will also be helping the environment. And we all want to live in a beautiful, healthy environment, don't we? ☐

2. Now write a **different conclusion** for Angelo's speech.

____

____

____

Writing the final draft

This is Angelo's **final draft**. Read the comments about his **speech** on the left, and do the tasks on the right.

Comments

Starting by ***acknowledging the audience*** *is a polite thing to do.*

Engaging *directly with the audience helps get their attention.*

Using ***connectives*** *links the arguments and helps make the writing flow.*

Using strong ***evidence*** *to support arguments makes them more effective.*

Using **modal verbs** *and* ***adverbs*** *shows how certain the speaker is of his arguments.*

Ending with a ***conclusion*** *that repeats the point of view and refers back to the arguments is an effective way to end the speech.*

We need more trees!

Good morning, Ms Johnson and students.

Imagine it is a really hot day. Where would you rather sit–on a bench in the blazing sun, or on the grass beneath a shady tree? I am sure you would all choose the shady tree. This is one reason I think we should spend the $1000 on trees for the school grounds, but there are others too.

Firstly, trees have important health benefits. They help reduce greenhouse gases by absorbing carbon dioxide, and they produce oxygen, which we all need to survive. Also, trees protect us from the harsh rays of the sun. If we sit or play in their shade, we are less likely to get burnt, and consequently will be less likely to develop diseases such as skin cancer.

Secondly, trees are good for the environment. They provide food and homes for a wide variety of birds, insects and small mammals. These animals have great benefits for the environment. Birds, for example, help with pest control by eating unwelcome visitors such as mosquitoes. They also play a key role in pollination, which is an important part of the life cycle of plants. If we plant more trees, we will be helping the environment by attracting more wildlife into the school grounds.

In addition, trees cool the atmosphere by releasing moisture into the air. In the hot summer months, therefore, more trees in the school grounds will not only protect us from the sun, but will also help keep us cool.

I hope my arguments have persuaded you that the $1000 should be spent on trees for the school grounds. Planting trees will not only add beauty and character to our school, but it will also help the environment. And you all want to live in a beautiful, healthy environment, don't you?

Tasks

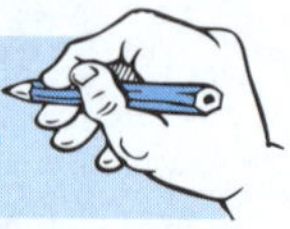

1. **Underline** the **general statement** of position.
2. **Circle** three **connectives**.
3. **Underline** a **sentence** that provides evidence of the importance of birds in the environment.
4. **Circle** two **connectives**.
5. **Underline** the **question**.

Student B: Lien's draft

Lien is also in Angelo's class. She believes the $1000 the Year 5s have raised should be spent on buying more books for the school library.

Before writing her **speech**, she also did some research to make sure she had strong arguments and evidence to support her position. These are the rough notes she made.

> value of books not like internet—can read a book wherever we are—encourage us to use our imaginations—contain lots of new words—contain reliable information—prevent us from becoming bored—have to visualise people, places and events—help us expand our vocabularies—publishers and editors check what people write

Fill in the missing information below.

Argument	Supporting evidence
1 Encourage us to use our imaginations	
2	Contain lots of new words
3 Contain reliable information	
4	Can read a book wherever you are

Writing the first draft

This is Lien's **first draft**. Read it and then answer the questions.

> I think we should spend the $1000 on more books for the school library. These are some of the reasons.
>
> Books encourage us to use our imaginations. We can't see the action taking place, so we have to visualise it.
>
> Books help us expand our vocabularies. Books usually contain words we haven't seen before, so by reading books, we learn new words.
>
> The information in books is more reliable than information on the internet. This is because publishers and editors check what people have written.

1 Which of these features has Lien remembered to use in her draft? Tick (✓) the correct answers.

- **a** an opening paragraph that contains the **statement of position** or **point of view**, plus some background information ☐
- **b** a series of **arguments** that give **reasons** for the point of view ☐
- **c** strong, detailed **evidence** to **support** the arguments ☐
- **d** a **conclusion** that **repeats** the point of view and **refers back** to the arguments ☐
- **e** **thinking and feeling verbs** ☐
- **f** **modal verbs** and **adverbs** ☐
- **g** **present-tense verbs** throughout ☐
- **h** **connectives** to link **arguments** ☐

2 Choose a **thinking** or **feeling verb** from the box to complete these sentences that Lien could add to her speech.

imagine	know	believe

- **a** I ______________ that books are the greatest friends we have.
- **b** ______________ a world without books!
- **c** I ______________ that if I have a book to read, I will never be lonely.

Step-by-step improvement plan

Lien also needs to work on her **speech** to make it more interesting and convincing. Help her complete these exercises to find ways to do this.

Step 1: Start with a good introduction

Use these phrases to construct a more interesting **introduction** for Lien's speech.

raised $1000 dollars

I believe

when I have given my reasons

what to spend it on

resources for the school

will agree with me

The question is

Step 2: Link ideas with connectives

Lien's speech will flow better if she uses connectives to link her arguments.

Underline the **connective** in brackets that correctly completes each sentence.

1. There are many things we could spend the $1000 on; (as long as/for instance), more plants for the gardens, new pathways and more computers for the classrooms.
2. I believe, (however/then), that the money should be spent on new books for the school library.
3. (In the first place/Apart from), when we read books, we have to use our imaginations.
4. Visualising the action encourages us to become more creative and, (nevertheless/consequently), better thinkers and writers.
5. (Despite/Furthermore), reading books can help us expand our vocabularies.
6. (Finally/Until), the information in books is usually reliable.

Step 3: Show certainty with modal verbs and adverbs

Lien can add authority to her arguments by including some modal verbs and adverbs.

Find a **modal verb** or **adverb** in the list to complete each of these sentences. The words in brackets will help you choose the correct word.

surely	perhaps	may	definitely	might not	must

1. We should ____________ buy more books for the library. (certain)
2. Having lots of new books in the library ____________ encourage some students to read more. (uncertain)
3. Compared to the internet, you will ____________ agree that books contain more reliable information. (certain)
4. We ____________ keep buying new books for the library if we want to keep it up to date. (certain)
5. Some people ________________ think that buying more books for the library is the best way to spend the money. (uncertain)
6. ____________ if I tell you how important books are, you will agree with me. (uncertain)

Step 4: End with a good conclusion

1. Which **conclusion** is more likely to impress Lien's audience?

A I hope that the arguments I have presented today will convince you that the $1000 should be spent on purchasing new books for the library. I know that some people would prefer to spend the money on new plants for the gardens, but as an old Chinese proverb reminds us: a book is like a garden in your pocket! ☐

B Books help us in so many ways. We all want to be better readers, thinkers and writers, don't we? The only way to achieve this is to read more books. That's why I vote for spending the $1000 on new books for the library! ☐

2. Now write a **different conclusion** for Lien's speech.

____

____

____

____

____

____

____

Writing the final draft

Lien has started writing the **final draft** of her **speech**. Help her complete it by filling in the missing sections, and then look in the answers section to compare what you have written with what she wrote.

Hint! Look at the practice exercises for ideas.

Good morning, Ms Johnson and students.

The Year 5s have raised $1000 dollars to spend on resources for the school. The question is—what should we spend it on? I believe we should use the money to buy new books for the school library, and when I have given you my reasons, I am sure you will agree with me.

Firstly, when we read books, we have to use our imaginations. Unlike movies and television programs, books don't show us what is happening—they tell us. **(Expand on this argument by explaining how books help us become more creative thinkers.)**

....

....

....

....

....

In addition, reading books can help us expand our vocabularies. **(Expand on this argument by explaining how having a good vocabulary can benefit us.)**

....

....

....

....

....

Finally, the information in books is usually reliable. **(Expand on this argument by comparing the information in books with information on the internet.)**

....

....

....

....

....

I hope that the arguments I have presented today will convince you that the $1000 should be spent on purchasing new books for the library. I know that some people would prefer to spend the money on new plants for the gardens, but as an old Chinese proverb reminds us: a book is like having a garden in your pocket!

Your turn

Write an **exposition** of one to two pages on one of the following. Use your own paper for this activity.

Writing Checklist Make sure your exposition includes: ✓

- an opening paragraph in which you **state** your **position** or **point of view**. ☐
- a **series of arguments** that give **reasons** for your point of view. ☐
- strong, detailed **evidence** to **support** the **arguments**. ☐
- a **conclusion** that **repeats** the point of view and **refers back** to the arguments. ☐
- **thinking** and **feeling verbs**. ☐
- **modal verbs** and **adverbs**. ☐
- **present-tense verbs**. ☐
- **connectives** to link **arguments**. ☐

Tip Use **Angelo's final draft** on page 42 and **Lien's final draft** on page 47 to help you write your exposition.

Go to WORD BANK page 135 for useful vocabulary

1. If your Year 5 group had raised $1000 for new resources for the school, what would you like to see the money spent on?

   Write a speech in which you give arguments to support your point of view. Use Angelo and Lien's speeches as models.

2. Write a speech in which you try to convince your classmates that eating and drinking foods that contain lots of sugar—such as lollies, cakes and soft drinks—is unhealthy.

   (You could argue that consuming too much sugar causes tooth decay, obesity and diseases such as diabetes.)

3. Write a letter to your local council complaining about the number of new high-rise buildings they are planning to construct in your suburb. Start your letter like this—

   Dear Mr Mayor

   My family and I are worried about the number of high-rises you are planning to build in. (*Give your suburb a name.*) In the local newspaper it states that some of these buildings could be up to 20 storeys high! We strongly believe that these high-rise developments will do our suburb more harm than good, for the following reasons. (*You could argue that the high-rises will block out the sun for people living in houses, and that lots more people will come to live in your suburb, making it more crowded and leading to an increase in traffic and pollution in the area.*)

4. Convince your parents that you need your own computer or tablet. Present your arguments in a letter.

Unit 5 Information reports

Looking at information reports

An **information report** provides factual information about a subject or topic. It usually describes a class or group of things, such as a type of animal, but sometimes it is about one thing only, such as a country.

Information reports can be about:

- plants and animals.
- technology (e.g. computers and motor cars).
- people, countries and cultures.

An **information report** should have:

- an **opening statement** that gives a **brief definition** or **description** of the subject, perhaps defining or classifying it.
- a series of **paragraphs** that give a more **detailed description** of the subject.
- a **conclusion** that rounds off the report.

Hint! **Diagrams** or **charts** may be included to support the text.

1 Tick (✓) the sentences that could be from an **information report**.

a Rainforests occur mainly along the east coast of Australia. ☐

b We spent an interesting day walking through the rainforest. ☐

c I can't imagine leaving home without my mobile phone! ☐

d Mobile phones can also be used to send and receive text messages. ☐

e Torres Strait Islanders are the indigenous people of the Torres Strait Islands, which are part of Queensland, Australia. ☐

f I have never been to the Torres Strait Islands, but that's where my friend comes from. ☐

2 Which of these is more likely to be the opening sentence of an **information report**?

a When mother penguins lose a chick, they sometimes try to steal another mother's chick. ☐

b Penguins are a group of aquatic, flightless birds. ☐

Student A: Arnon's draft

Arnon's Year 5 class is learning about the climatic regions of Australia. They have to write an **information report** about an animal that is found in *one* of the climatic zones. Arnon is going to write about the southern cassowary, which is found in the rainforests of northern Australia. First, Arnon researched the southern cassowary. He collected photographs of the bird and jotted down facts about its appearance, diet, behaviour, and so on.

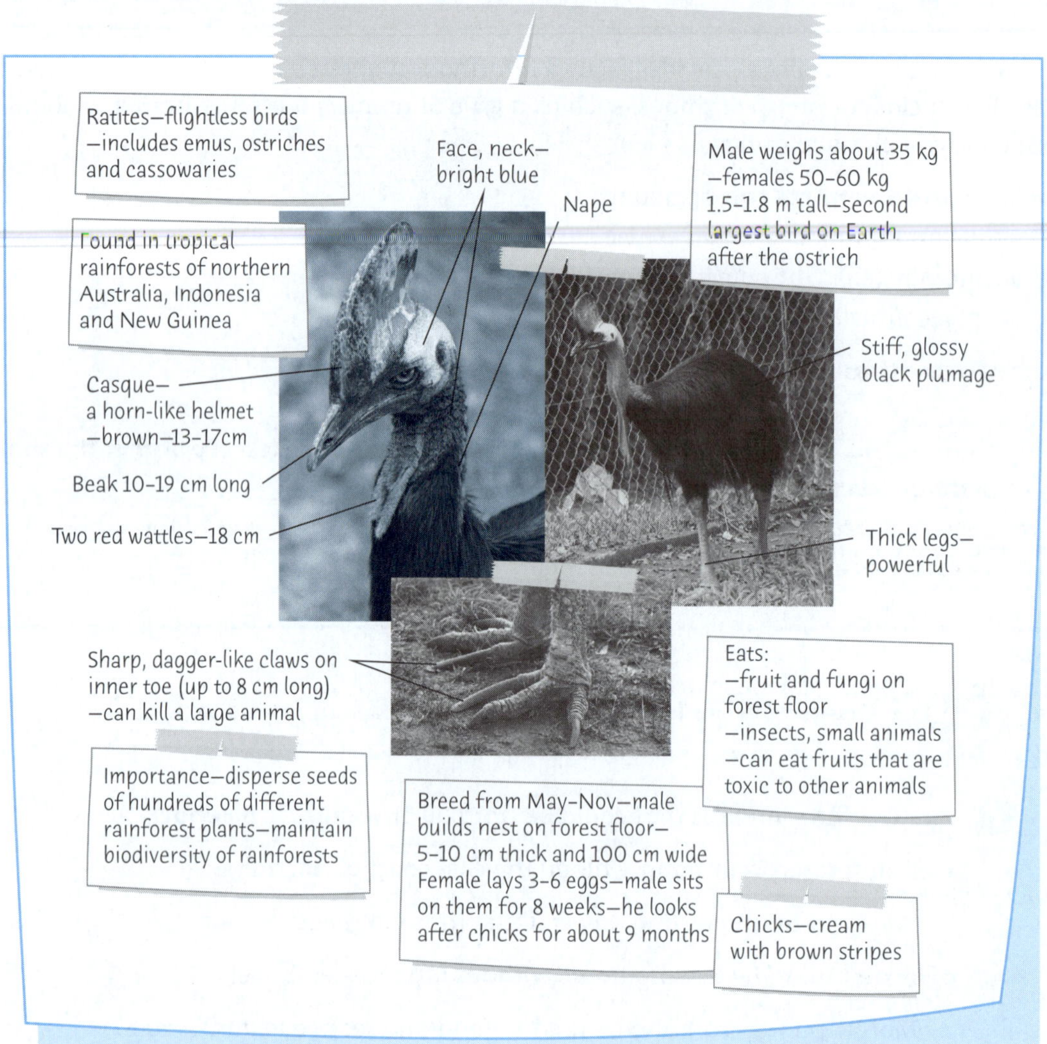

1. Help Arnon organise his information by writing **key words** and **phrases** next to these headings.

   Appearance: ______________________

   Size: ______________________

   Diet: ______________________

   Breeding: ______________________

2. Suggest two ways in which the southern cassowary might defend itself.

   ____

   ____

Writing the first draft

This is Arnon's **first draft**. Read what he wrote and then answer the questions.

The Southern Cassowary

The southern cassowary is a large bird. I think it is the most fascinating bird in Australia.

Its feathers are black and its face is blue. Two red folds of skin hang from its throat. It has a helmet on its head and quite a long beak.

The southern cassowary has thick legs and feet. It has a claw on one of its toes. It uses the claw to defend itself. It's also got a strong kick.

The female cassowary is usually heavier than the male.

The southern cassowary eats fruit, fungi, insects and other small animals.

The male builds the nest. He sits on the eggs until they hatch and then he looks after the chicks. I think it's unfair that the female makes the male do all the work.

The southern cassowary is found in the tropical rainforests of northern Australia, Indonesia and New Guinea. I think I'd like to go to a rainforest to see one.

Southern cassowaries are important because they help spread the seeds of hundreds of different plants around the rainforest.

1 A good **information report** should contain the following features. Tick (✓) the ones that Arnon has used.

- **a** an **opening statement** that contains a **classification**, **definition** or **brief description** of the subject ☐
- **b** a **detailed description** of the subject presented in a **series** of **paragraphs** ☐
- **c** a **conclusion** that **rounds off** the report ☐
- **d** **well-structured paragraphs** that contain a **topic sentence** or **heading** that tells the reader what the paragraph is about (e.g. *The southern cassowary eats a varied diet.*) ☐
- **e** only **facts**, not opinions ☐
- **f** **technical language** (e.g. *plumage, wattles*) ☐
- **g** **present-tense verbs** (e.g. *is, are, has*) ☐
- **h** **sentences** with **correct spelling** and **punctuation** ☐

2 List seven **adjectives** that Arnon has used in the first two paragraphs of his draft.

____

____

Step-by-step improvement plan

Arnon's report is fairly informative and interesting, but there are a number of ways in which he can improve his draft. The following exercises contain tips on how he can do this. Help him complete them.

Step 1: Start with a good opening statement

The **opening statement** is the first paragraph of the report. It should contain enough **information** about the topic to make the reader want to find out more, without being too long.

Arnon's opening statement does not include enough information about the southern cassowary to make the reader want to find out more about the bird. It also contains an unnecessary opinion.

Use the information in Arnon's notes to write a better **opening statement** for his report. Make sure you include the words *ratite, flightless, ostriches* and *emus*.

____

____

____

____

____

Step 2: Use topic sentences to write well-structured paragraphs

A **topic sentence** is a sentence that contains the **main idea** of a paragraph. The other sentences in the paragraph should relate to the topic sentence in some way. The topic sentence usually appears at the beginning of the paragraph.

Using a topic sentence lets the reader know **what** the paragraph is about. It also helps structure the paragraph.

Arnon's paragraphs lack structure because they do not contain topic sentences.

1 Tick (✓) the sentence that would make a good **topic sentence** for the paragraph about the

a appearance of the southern cassowary.

i The southern cassowary has a distinctive appearance. ☐

ii The southern cassowary is black, blue and red. ☐

b way the cassowary defends itself.

i The cassowary has powerful legs and a sharp claw. ☐

ii The cassowary has two main weapons with which to defend itself. ☐

2 Now write a **topic sentence** for the paragraph about the

a size of the cassowary. ______________________________

____

b breeding habits of the cassowary. ______________________________

____

Step 3: Use technical language

Technical language is language that is **specific** to a **particular subject**.

For example: *Ratite* is a word that relates specifically to flightless birds like the southern cassowary.

Using technical language in an information report makes it sound more formal and authoritative. It also helps build information about the subject.

Use Arnon's notes to construct a sentence with each of these **technical words** that relate specifically to the southern cassowary.

1. wattles: ____________________

2. casque: ____________________

Step 4: State facts, not opinions

A **fact** is something that can be proved to be true.

For example: Most birds can fly.

An **opinion** is a personal view that may or may not be true.

For example: All baby birds are ugly.

An information report should contain only facts, not opinions.

1. Which sentence is an **opinion**? Tick (✓) the correct answer.
   - **a** The southern cassowary is a large, flightless bird. ☐
   - **b** The southern cassowary is the most beautiful bird in the rainforest. ☐
2. Underline all the **opinions** that Arnon has expressed in his draft.
3. Now write a good sentence about the southern cassowary with each of the following words. Your sentences must be **facts**, not **opinions**. Use Arnon's notes to help you.

Note: you need to write different sentences from the ones Arnon has used in his draft.

For example: plumage—The southern cassowary is covered in stiff, glossy black plumage.

- **a** claw ____________________
- **b** fruits ____________________
- **c** nest ____________________

Writing the final draft

This is Arnon's **final draft**. Read the comments about his **report** on the left, and do the tasks on the right.

Comments

Starting with a good ***opening statement*** *engages the reader's interest and makes them want to find out more.*

Starting a paragraph with a ***topic sentence*** *helps give structure to a paragraph and tells the reader what the paragraph is about.*

Using ***technical language*** *adds important information and makes the writing sound formal and authoritative.*

Using ***facts****, not opinions, gives the reader reliable information about southern cassowaries.*

The ***conclusion*** *rounds off the report with a final statement about the importance of the southern cassowary.*

The Southern Cassowary

The southern cassowary belongs to the ratite group of birds. Ratites are large, flightless birds that include ostriches and emus.

The southern cassowary has a distinctive appearance. Its body is covered in stiff, glossy black plumage (feathers) and its face and neck are a bright blue with red colouring at the nape. Two red wattles (fleshy folds of skin), each measuring between 17 and 18 cm, hang from its throat. On top of its head is a brown, horn-like helmet called a casque, which can be anywhere from 13 to 17 cm high.

The southern cassowary's main weapons are its thick legs and feet. Each foot has three toes, with a sharp, dagger-like claw on the inner toe. The claws can be up to 8 cm long and are capable of killing large animals. The southern cassowary also has a very powerful kick.

The southern cassowary is the second-largest bird on Earth after the ostrich. The female cassowary is generally heavier than the male, weighing in at between 50 and 60 kg, while the male weighs on average 35 kg. Cassowaries are anywhere from 1.5 to 1.8 m tall.

The southern cassowary eats a varied diet. It feeds on fruit that it finds on the forest floor, fungi (such as mushrooms), insects and other small animals. The cassowary can safely eat fruits that are toxic (poisonous) to other animals.

Southern cassowaries breed between May and November. It is the male's job to build the nest. He uses plant material to construct a soft bed that is about 5 to 10 cm thick and up to 100 cm wide. The female lays three to six eggs and the male sits on them for about eight weeks until they hatch. The chicks, which are cream with brown stripes, stay with the male for nine months.

The southern cassowary is found in the tropical rainforests of northern Australia, Indonesia and New Guinea.

Cassowaries are responsible for dispersing the seeds of hundreds of different rainforest plants. These birds therefore play an important role in maintaining the biodiversity of our tropical rainforests.

Tasks

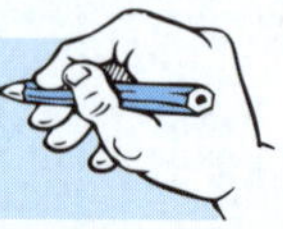

1. **Underline** the **technical word** that relates specifically to flightless birds.
2. **Underline** the **topic sentence**.
3. **Circle** the **adjectives** that describe the southern cassowary's claw.
4. **Underline** a **fact** about the height of a southern cassowary.
5. **Circle** four **adjectives**.
6. **Underline** the **topic sentence**.
7. **Circle** the **proper nouns**.
8. **Underline** three **abstract nouns**.

Student B: Sabita's draft

Sabita, another Year 5 student, is going to write an **information report** about the Greengrocer cicada, which is found in the temperate region of Australia's east coast, between southern Queensland and Victoria and South Australia.

Sabita also started by collecting photographs and information about the insect.

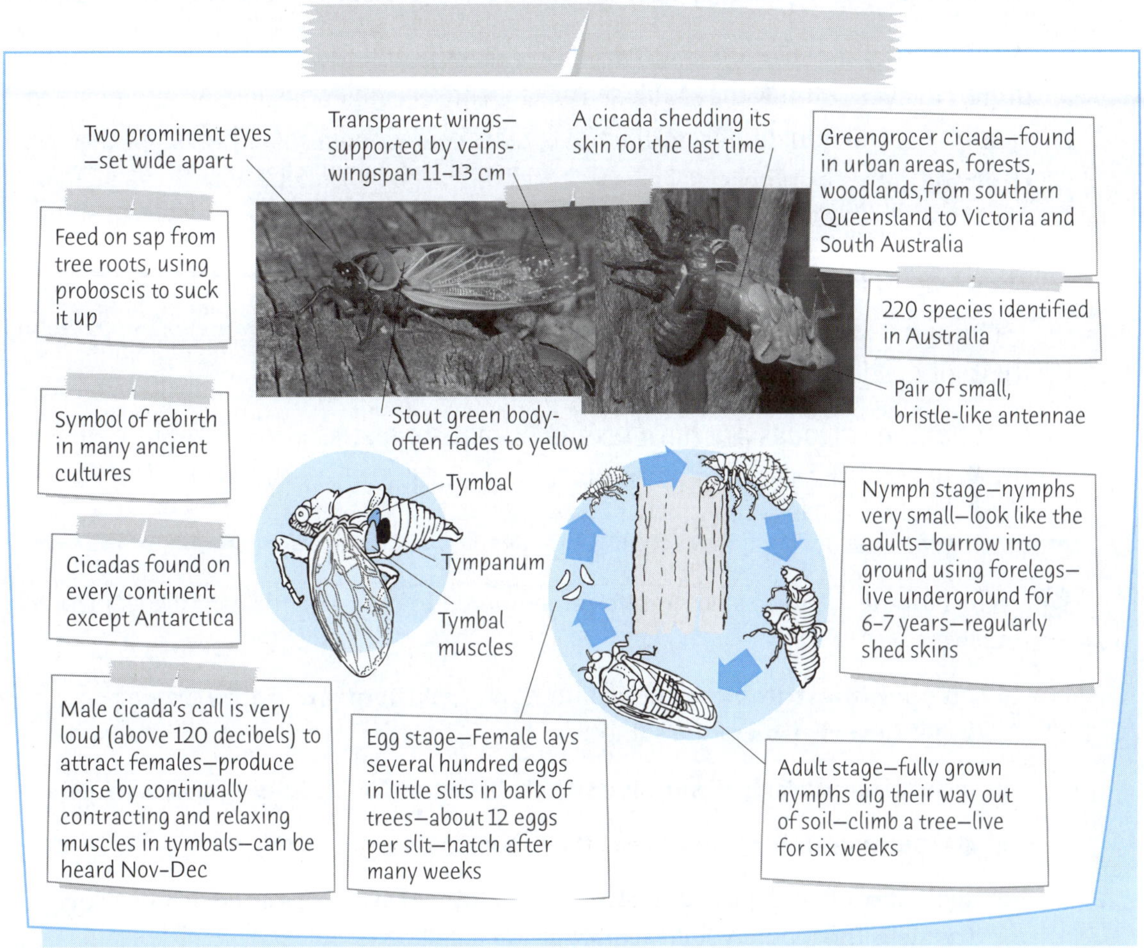

1. Help Sabita organise the information about the cicada's life cycle by writing **key words** in the boxes.

Life cycle of the Greengrocer cicada

Egg stage	Nymph stage	Adult stage
______	______	______
______	______	______
______	______	______
______	______	______

2. In which season can the cicada's shrill call be heard?

____

Writing the first draft

This is Sabita's **first draft**. Read it and then answer the questions.

> ## The Greengrocer cicada
>
> **Introduction**: The Greengrocer cicada is a small insect with a very loud call.
>
> **Appearance**: It has a small, green body, six legs and two pairs of wings. It has quite big eyes. I think they look scary. Greengrocer cicadas live on the eastern side of Australia in cities and towns, forests and woodlands. They suck the sap from the stems of plants.
>
> **Life cycle**: When the eggs hatch, the babies burrow their way into the ground. They live underground for six or seven years. When they are fully grown, they come to the surface again. The adult males use muscles in their bodies to make their loud, shrill call. They do it to attract females.
>
> Greengrocer cicadas are harmless to humans because they don't bite or sting. I think that their call could harm our ears though. It is very loud!

1 Which of these features has Sabita remembered to use in her draft? Tick (✓) the correct answers.

- **a** an **opening statement** that contains a **classification**, **definition** or **brief description** of the subject ☐
- **b** a **detailed description** of the subject presented as a **series** of **paragraphs** ☐
- **c** a **conclusion** that **rounds off** the report in a factual way ☐
- **d** **well-structured paragraphs** that contain a **topic sentence** or **heading** that tells the reader what the paragraph is about ☐
- **e** only **facts**, not opinions ☐
- **f** **technical language** ☐
- **g** **present-tense verbs** ☐

2 Write a sentence that Sabita could add about the following topics.

a the wings of the Greengrocer cicada

____

____

b the number of cicada species identified in Australia

____

____

Step-by-step improvement plan

Sabita clearly needs to do some work on her draft to turn it into an interesting **information report**. She is going to do some practice exercises to find ideas on how to do this. Help her complete them.

Step 1: Start with a good opening statement

Like Arnon's opening statement, Sabita's does not contain enough information to engage the reader's interest. Rewrite her **introduction** and add two more sentences. Use the information in her notes to help you.

Step 2: Write well-structured paragraphs

The information in Sabita's paragraphs is not always about the topic indicated by her heading.

For example: in the paragraph about the cicada's appearance, Sabita has included information that has nothing to do with the way it looks.

1. Read Sabita's draft again and underline the two sentences that do not belong under the heading *Appearance*.
2. Write 1 to 2 sentences for each of the following headings that Sabita could use in her report. Use her notes to help you find the information.

Habitat:

Feeding:

Step 3: Use technical language

By adding **technical language** to her report, Sabita will be able to build information and make her report sound more authoritative.

1. Replace each of the words below with a more **technical term** from the box.

nymphs	abdomens	antennae

a feelers ____________ b babies ____________ c bodies ____________

2. Now use Sabita's notes to help you make a sentence with each of the new words.

a nymphs ____

____

b abdomens ____

____

c antennae ____

____

Step 4: State facts, not opinions

1. Like Arnon, Sabita has made the mistake of adding personal **opinions** to her report. Find them in her draft and underline them.

2. Which of these sentences is Sabita's **opinion** about the Greengrocer cicada's call? Tick (✓) the correct answer.

a The Greengrocer cicada makes a loud, high-pitched call. ☐

b The Greengrocer cicada has the worst insect call I have ever heard. ☐

3. Use the labelled diagram from Sabita's notes (page 56) to write a paragraph about how the male Greengrocer cicada makes its loud, high-pitched call. Do not include any **opinions** in your description. Your paragraph should include the words *organs, tymbals, abdomens, muscles, contracting* and *relaxing*.

____

____

____

____

____

____

____

____

Writing the final draft

Sabita has started writing the **final draft** of her **information report**. Help her complete it and then look in the answers section to compare what you have written with what she wrote.

Hint! Look at the practice exercises and Sabita's notes for ideas.

The Greengrocer cicada

The cicada is a small insect that is found on every continent except Antarctica. In Latin its name means *tree cricket*. The Greengrocer cicada, which is one of the loudest insects in the world, is just one of the 220 species of cicada that have been identified in Australia.

Appearance

....

....

....

....

....

Habitat and Distribution

The Greengrocer cicada lives in urban areas, forests and woodlands along the eastern side of Australia between southern Queensland and Victoria and South Australia.

Feeding

....

....

Life cycle

Egg stage: After mating, the female lays several hundred eggs in little slits that she makes in the bark of trees. She deposits about twelve eggs in each slit. After many weeks, the eggs hatch and the nymphs emerge.

Nymph stage: The nymphs are very small, but have the same appearance as adult cicadas. They drop to the ground and, using their large forelegs, burrow into the earth. They use the sharp, needle-like projections at the top of their heads to suck the sap from the roots of trees. They continue to grow underground for a period of between six and seven years, regularly shedding their skins.

Adult stage: When the nymph is fully grown, it digs its way out of the soil and climbs onto a tree trunk. Here it sheds its skin for the last time. It lives for about six weeks on the surface, during which time it mates and lays its eggs for the cycle to start again.

Communication

....

....

....

Interesting facts
Cicadas are harmless to humans as they do not bite or sting. In ancient times they were condidered to be a symbol of rebirth because of the way they emerged from the soil.

Your turn

Write an **information report** of one to two pages on one of the following. Use your own paper for this activity.

Writing Checklist Make sure your information report includes: ✓

- an **opening statement** that contains a **classification**, **definition** or **brief description** of the subject. ☐
- a **detailed description** of the subject presented as a **series** of **paragraphs**. ☐
- a **conclusion** that **rounds off** the report. ☐
- **well-structured paragraphs** that contain a **topic sentence** or **heading** that tells the reader what the paragraph is about. ☐ ☐
- **facts**, not opinions. ☐
- **technical language**. ☐
- **present-tense verbs**. ☐
- sentences that have the **correct spelling** and **punctuation**. ☐

Tip Use **Arnon's final draft** on page 54 and **Sabita's final draft** on page 59 to help you write your report.

Go to WORD BANK page 135 for useful vocabulary

1. Research an animal that is native to Australia and then write your findings as an information report. Use Arnon and Sabita's reports as models.
2. Use the information below plus your own research notes to write a report about the platypus.

Platypus
looks like a cross between an otter, beaver and duck—good swimmer

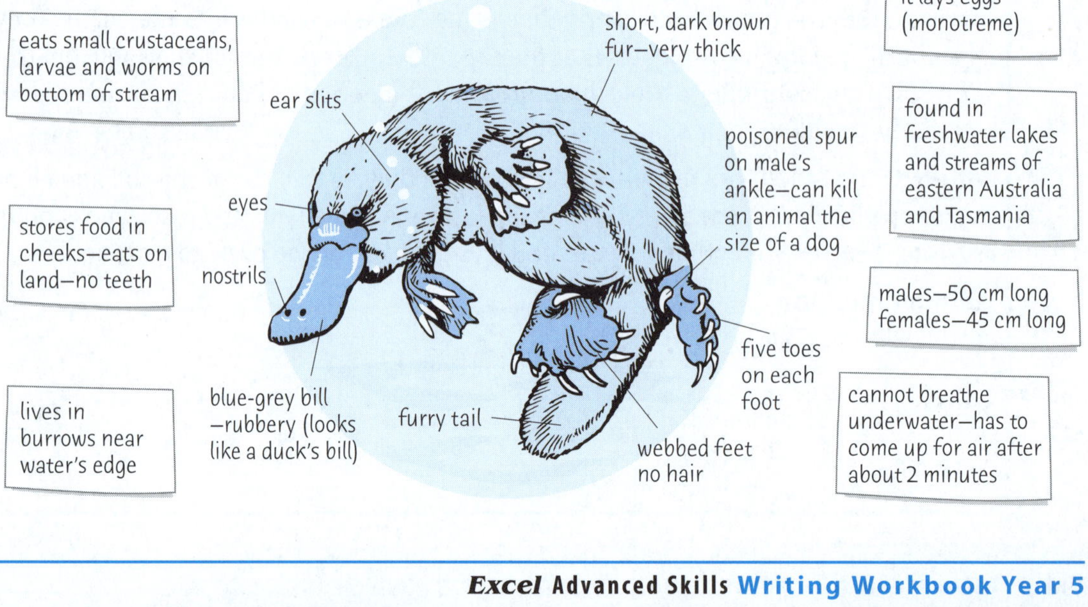

Unit 6 Procedures—video presentations

Looking at procedures

A **procedure** is a **factual** text. It gives instructions on how to **make** or **do** something.

Texts such as recipes, science experiments and manuals on how to play a game or put together a model are examples of procedures.

The main **purpose** of a procedure is to provide **sequenced information** or **directions** so that people can perform a task safely and efficiently.

A **procedure** should have:

- an **opening statement** that tells what the aim or purpose of the procedure is.
- a **list** of the ingredients, materials or equipment that will be needed.
- a **series of steps** or instructions, given in the correct order.
- a **concluding statement** or comment to wrap up the procedure. (This is not always necessary.)

Hint! Photographs, drawings or diagrams are often included to support the text.

1. Which of the following could be written as a **procedure**? Tick (✓) the correct answer.

   a telling about a movie you have seen ☐

   b explaining how to make a salad sandwich ☐

   c thanking someone for a gift ☐

   d giving directions on how to get from one place to another ☐

   e warning about the dangers of smoking ☐

2. Which of the texts below is a **procedure**? Tick (✓) the correct answer.

   a Spread glue on the back of the card. Position the card in the centre of the page. Stick it down firmly. ☐

   b I thought the card would look perfect in the centre of the page. All I needed was some glue. ☐

Student A: Livia's draft

Livia's Year 5 class are reading *Harry Potter and the Philosopher's Stone*.
Each group in the class has to make something that relates to the novel in some way. They are going to make a video of the procedure to show the class afterwards. Livia's group is going to make a shadow puppet theatre with shadow puppets that look like the characters from the novel. Livia is going to write the **procedure** that gives instructions on how to do this.

Before she gets started, Livia organises her information by drawing some diagrams and making notes.

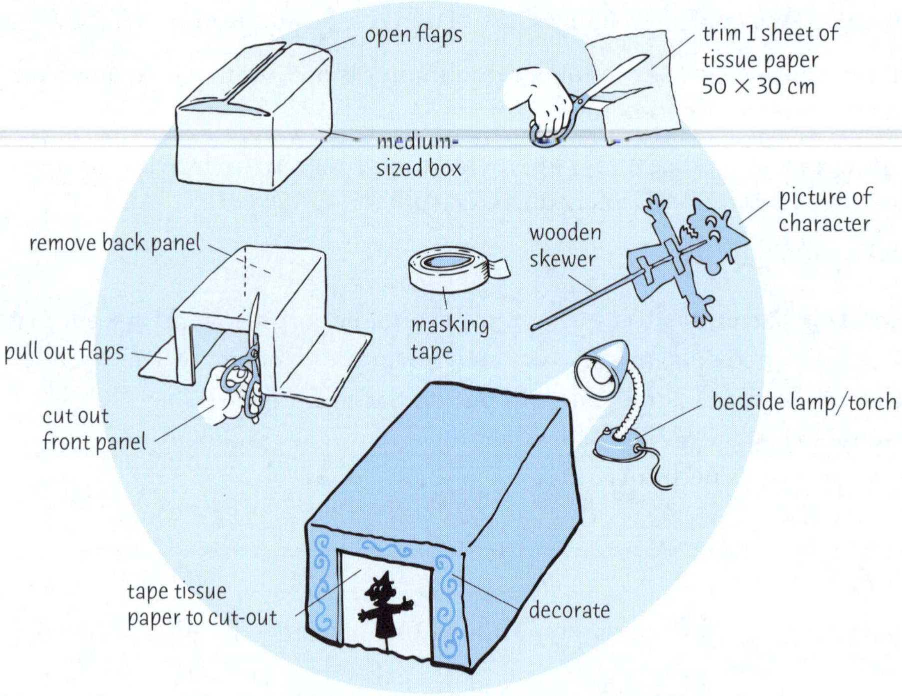

1. Write down all the **nouns** that Livia has used in her notes.

2. Write down all the **verbs** that Livia has used in her notes.

Writing the first draft

This is Livia's **first draft**. Read what she wrote and then answer the questions.

> **Materials needed:** 1 cardboard box (50 × 30 cm), scissors, white tissue paper, masking tape, lamp, pictures of characters, black craft paper, wooden skewers, glue
>
> **Steps:**
>
> You must cut off the top and back of the box and cut out a section in the front for a screen.
>
> If you pull out the two side flaps you can make the box stand.
>
> You can use tissue paper for a screen.
>
> You can find pictures of the characters on the internet. Just trace them or stick them onto the craft paper and cut them out. It is easy to hold them if you stick them onto skewers. The lamp goes behind the box.

1 A good **procedure** should contain the following features. Tick (✓) the ones that Livia has used.

- **a** an **opening statement** that includes the **aim** or **purpose** of the procedure ☐
- **b** a **list** of the **ingredients** or materials that will be needed ☐
- **c** a clear **series of steps**, or **instructions**, given in the **correct order** ☐
- **d** a **concluding statement** or comment that **wraps up** the procedure ☐
- **e** **sentences** that **start** with **action verbs** (e.g. **Remove** *the top flaps*, **Trim** *a piece of tissue paper to fit the screen*) ☐
- **f** **connectives** that show **sequence** (e.g. *first*, *after that*); sequence can also be shown by numbering the steps ☐
- **g** **adverbs** and **adverbial phrases** that tell **how**, **where** and **when** an action is performed (e.g. *Cut* **carefully**, *Turn the box* **on its side**) ☐
- **h** **detailed instructions** that are **clearly expressed** ☐
- **i** **sentences** with **correct spelling** and **punctuation** ☐

2 Livia has used some adverbial phrases in her draft.

> **Reminder!** Adverbial phrases usually start with a preposition.
>
> For example: **on** *its side*.

Read Livia's draft again and underline the **adverbial phrase** that tells where:

- **a** you should cut out a section for a screen.
- **b** you can find pictures of the characters.
- **c** you can stick the pictures.
- **d** the lamp goes.

Step-by-step improvement plan

There are a number of areas Livia needs to work on to improve her draft. She is going to do some practice exercises to find ways to do this. Help her complete them.

Step 1: Start with an interesting opening statement

The **opening statement** is the introduction. Its main purpose is to state as clearly as possible the **aim** of the procedure.

Hint! Most procedures do not use words to capture the reader's attention. In some cases, however, attention-grabbing words can add interest to the introduction.

Livia's draft does not have an opening statement, so she has asked the other members in her group for their ideas on what it should contain. This is what they had to say.

I think we should say something about how using a shadow puppet theatre and shadow puppets to act out scenes from the novel can help bring the characters to life.

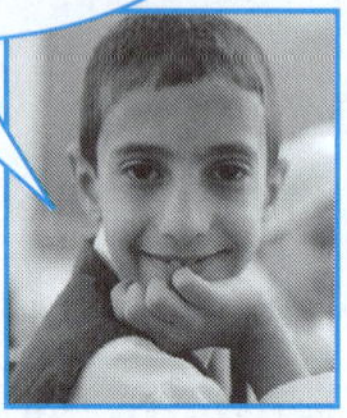

Ruben

I think it's important to mention that we are going to show everyone how to make a shadow puppet theatre and shadow puppets.

Cindy

I think we should add something about how easy it is to make a shadow puppet theatre and shadow puppets.

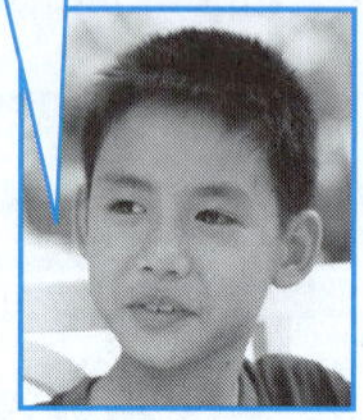

Danny

Now put the group's ideas together to create an **opening statement** for Livia's procedure.

____

____

____

____

Step 2: Start sentences with action verbs

Action verbs tell what is to be done (e.g. *find, cut, draw*). Placing the action verb at the beginning of the sentence emphasises the action, making the instruction easier to understand.

Livia's instructions are clumsy and difficult to follow because she has used the pronoun *you* in front of the action verb.

Write sentences for Livia's procedure that start with these **action verbs**.

1. Remove ______________________________
2. Turn ______________________________
3. Tape ______________________________
4. Decorate ______________________________

Step 3: Use connectives to sequence information

Connectives show the sequence of events or actions to be performed. In a procedure in which the steps are not numbered, connectives create a smooth link from one instruction to the next.

If you are using connectives, they should come before the action verb at the beginning of the sentence.

For example: **First** remove the top flaps.

Livia has not numbered her steps, nor has she used **connectives** to link the instructions.

Use a connective from the box to link the instructions below so that the sequence is clear.

After that	Finally	Eventually	First
Next	Meanwhile	Before	Then

1. ____________, look for pictures of the characters on the internet.
2. ____________, trace them onto black craft paper.
3. ____________, cut out the figures, making sure you get into the corners.
4. ____________, tape the figures onto wooden skewers.

Step 4: End with a good concluding statement

The **concluding statement** should wrap up the procedure in some way; for example, at the end of a recipe the concluding statement might be: *This delicious dessert will have everyone coming back for seconds.*

Livia's draft does not contain a concluding statement, so once again, she has asked the other members in her group for ideas.

Ruben—*I think we should say something about the hours of fun people can have with a shadow puppet theatre.*

Cindy—*Perhaps we can say something like: "Let the show begin!"*

Danny—*I think it's important to remind people how easy it is to make.*

What do *you* think Livia should say in her concluding statement?

____

____

____

____

____

Writing the final draft

This is Livia's **final draft**. Read the comments about her **procedure** on the left, and do the tasks on the right.

Comments

Starting with an interesting **opening statement** *gets the viewer's attention and lets them know exactly what you are going to do.*

Starting sentences with **action verbs** *emphasises the action, making the instruction clearer and easier to understand.*

Using **time connectives** *helps sequence the information and makes the instructions easier to follow.*

Using **adverbs** *and* **adverbial phrases** *adds important details about how, where or when an action should be performed.*

Adding the **concluding statement** *wraps up the procedure.*

How to make a shadow puppet theatre

Acting out scenes from the novel using a shadow puppet theatre and shadow puppets is a great way to make the characters come to life. Making a shadow puppet theatre is really easy. Just follow these simple steps.

Materials needed: 1 cardboard box (50 × 30 cm), scissors, white tissue paper, masking tape, lamp, pictures of characters, black craft paper, wooden skewers, glue

Steps:

First, remove the top flaps and back panel from a medium sized cardboard box. You can use scissors to do this.

Next, turn the box over and pull out the side flaps so that the box stands securely.

Then, cut out a section for the screen at the front of the box.

Cut and trim a piece of tissue paper and tape it to the inside of the box so that it covers the screen.

Meanwhile, find pictures of the characters from the novel on the internet and print them out.

Trace the pictures onto black craft paper and cut them out carefully.

Finally, tape the pictures onto wooden skewers so that they are easy to hold.

When you are ready to present your play, plug in the lamp and position it so that the light shines in through the back of the box.

Let the show begin!

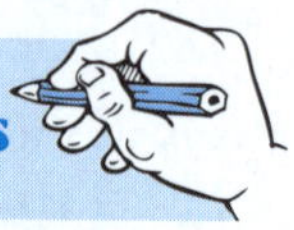

Tasks

1. **Underline** the **sentence** that is most likely to capture the viewer's attention.
2. **Underline** the **time connective.**
3. **Circle** three **action verbs.**
4. **Underline** the **time connective.**
5. **Circle** four **action verbs.**
6. **Underline** the **adverbial phrase** that tells where to find the pictures.
7. **Circle** the **time connective.**
8. **Underline** the **adverbial phrase** that tells where the light shines in.

Student B: Lucas's draft

Lucas's group likes the idea of Professor Snape's polyjuice potion, which, if you drink it, can make you look like somebody else. They are going to show the class how to make the polyjuice potion, and Lucas is going to write the **procedure** to go with their video.

Like Livia, Lucas starts by organising his information with drawings and notes.

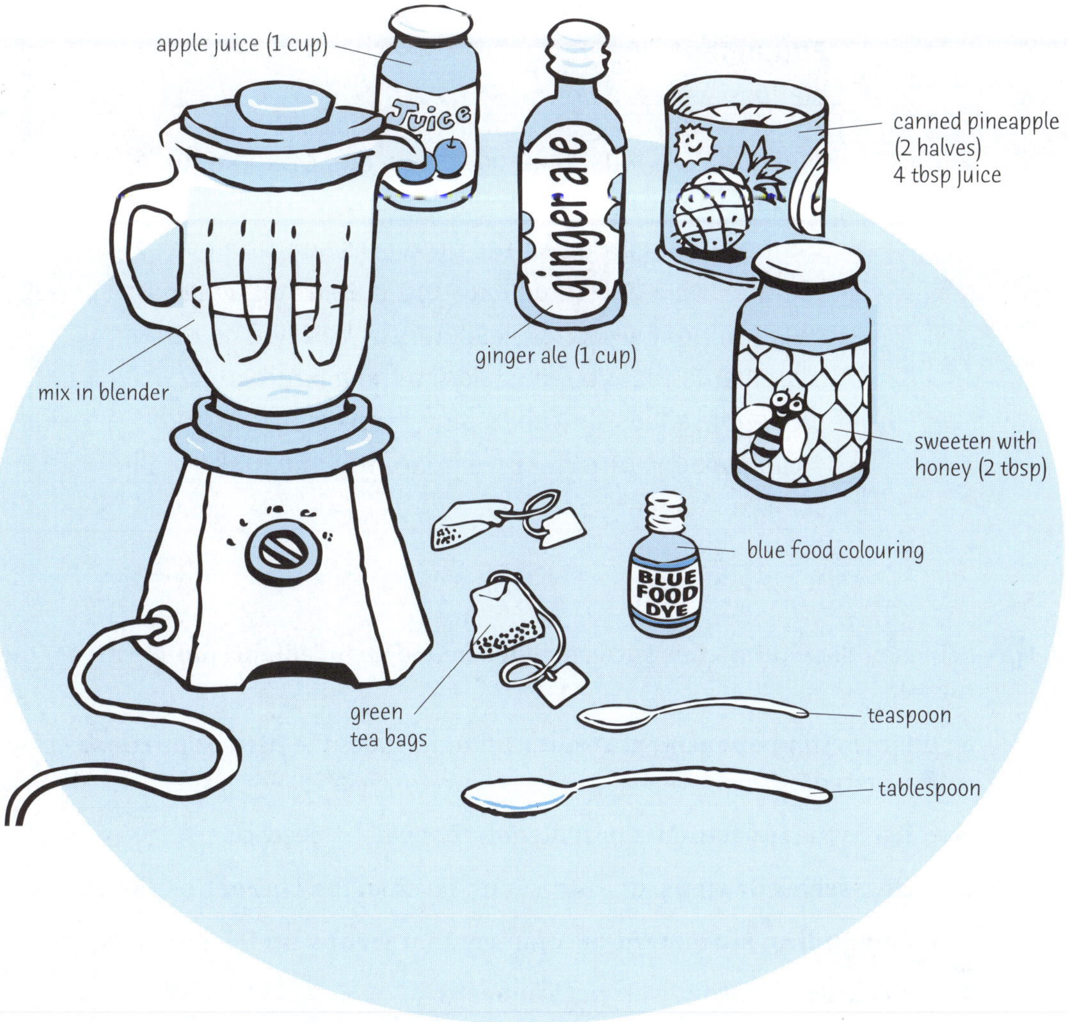

1. Write down all the **compound nouns** that Lucas has used in his notes. Remember that a compound noun is a noun that consists of two or more words.

2. Write down the **verbs** that Lucas has used.

Writing the first draft

This is Lucas's **first draft**. Read it and then answer the questions.

Recipe for polyjuice potion

Ingredients: apple juice, canned pineapples, ginger ale, blue food colouring, 2 green tea bags, hot water, honey

Equipment: cup, teaspoon, tablespoon, safety knife, blender, 2 plastic bowls

Method: You must mix together a cup of apple juice, a cup of ginger ale and 3 tablespoons of green tea solution. You can make the green tea solution by soaking the 2 green tea bags in 1 cup of hot water and sweetening it with 2 tablespoons of honey. The other ingredients that you must add to the mixture are 2 halved pineapple slices, 1 drop of blue food colouring and 4 tablespoons of pineapple juice. You can make it all smooth in a blender.

1 Which of these things has Lucas remembered to include in his draft? Tick (✓) the correct answers.

- **a** an interesting **opening statement** that includes the **aim** or **purpose** of the procedure ☐
- **b** a **list** of the **ingredients** or materials that will be needed ☐
- **c** a clear **series of steps**, or instructions, given in the **correct order** ☐
- **d** a **concluding statement** or comment that **wraps up** the procedure ☐
- **e** **sentences** that **start** with **action verbs** ☐
- **f** **connectives** or numbers to show the **order** in which the **actions** should be done ☐
- **g** **adverbs** and **adverbial phrases** that tell **how**, **where** and **when** an **action** is performed ☐
- **h** detailed **instructions** that are **clearly expressed** ☐

2 Like Livia, Lucas has used adverbial phrases to add detail to his sentences. Highlight the **adverbial phrase** that tells the following.

- **a** where you should soak the green tea bags
- **b** how the green tea solution can be sweetened
- **c** where you can make the potion smooth

Step-by-step improvement plan

Lucas is also going to do some practice exercises to turn his draft into a well-structured, clearly expressed **procedure**. Help him complete them.

Step 1: Start with an opening statement

Lucas's draft does not contain an opening statement, so, like Livia, he has turned to the other members of his group for help. They have decided that asking a question and then answering it would be a good way to start.

Complete this **opening statement** that Lucas's group is working on.

Would you like ______________________________? Well, ____________________

____

____________________. Just follow these simple instructions to create ________________

____

____

____

Step 2: Start sentences with action verbs

Lucas has also used the pronoun *you* in front of the action verbs.

Write the **instruction** that might go with each of the following pictures. Remember to start each sentence with an **action verb**.

a ____

b ____

c ____

Step 3: Use connectives to sequence information

Lucas has also decided not to use numbers to sequence the instructions, so he will have to use some **connectives** to make his procedure easier to follow.

Start each of these sentences with a suitable connective and complete them with the correct detail. Use Lucas's draft to help you.

1. ____________, soak 2 tea bags in ______________________________________.
2. ____________, sweeten the tea with ____________________________________.
3. ____________, pour a cup of apple juice and a cup of ginger ale into a plastic bowl.
4. Stir well.
5. ____________, add 2 halved pineapple slices to a blender, followed by 4 tablespoons ____.
6. Blend until ____.
7. ____________, combine all the ingredients in a large plastic bowl.

Step 4: End with a good concluding statement

Lucas's draft does not contain a **concluding statement** so, like Livia, he has asked the other members of his group for ideas.

What do *you* think Lucas should say in his concluding statement? Put together your ideas with those of the group and write a good concluding statement for Lucas's procedure.

____

____

____

____

____

____

Writing the final draft

Lucas has started writing the **final draft** of his **procedure**. Help him complete it, and then look in the answers section to compare what you have written with what Lucas wrote.

Hint! Look at Lucas's notes and the practice exercises for ideas.

Introduction:

Ingredients: apple juice, canned pineapples, ginger ale, blue food colouring, 2 green tea bags, hot water, honey

Equipment: cup, teaspoon, tablespoon, safety knife, blender, 2 plastic bowls

Method:

Conclusion:

....

....

....

....

....

Your turn

Write a **procedure** of one to two pages on one of the following. Use your own paper for this activity.

Writing Checklist Make sure your procedure includes: ✓

- an interesting **opening statement** that includes the **aim** or **purpose** of the procedure. ☐
- a **list** of the **ingredients** or **materials** that will be needed. ☐
- a clear **series of steps**, or instructions, given in the **correct order**. ☐
- a **concluding statement** or comment that **wraps up** the procedure. ☐
- **sentences** that **start** with **action verbs**. ☐
- **connectives** or numbers to show the **order** in which the **actions** should be done. ☐
- **adverbs** and **adverbial phrases** that tell **how**, **where** and **when** an **action** is performed. ☐

Tip Use **Livia's final draft** on page 66 and **Lucas's final draft** on page 71 to help you write your procedure.

Go to WORD BANK page 135 for useful vocabulary

1. Write a procedure that tells how to make something that is related to a novel you have read or are reading. Use Livia and Lucas's procedures as models.
2. Use these diagrams and notes to help you write a procedure that tells how the puppet is made.

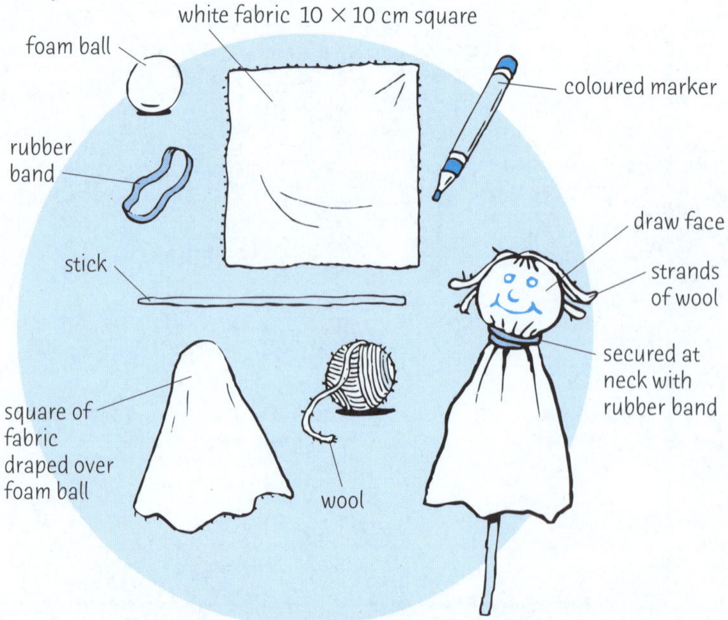

Unit 7 Poetry—ballads

Looking at ballads

A **ballad** is a poem that tells a **story**. It has a regular rhythm, or beat, and a definite rhyme pattern.

Long ago ballads told stories based on folk tales and legends. They were often set to music and performed by singers called minstrels. At a time when very few people could read, they were a way of passing down local tales from one generation to the next.

A **ballad** should

- tell a **story**.
- be divided into **stanzas**, or **verses**, usually consisting of four lines each.
- follow a **pattern** in which the last word in lines 2 and 4 **rhyme**.
- have a regular **rhythm**, with three stressed **syllables** in each line.
- **repeat** certain lines.

Hint! While not all ballads stick to this formula, they all tell a story and they all have a strong rhythm and rhyme scheme.

1. Which of the following verses has the stronger **rhythm**? Tick (✓) the correct answer.

Hint! Clapping your hands as you read the words will help you find the answer!

a

Tiger! Tiger! burning bright
In the forests of the night,
What immortal hand or eye
Could frame thy fearful symmetry? ☐

b

A raindrop landed
On a little leaf
On which fed a caterpillar.
He continued feeding unperturbed. ☐

2. Which of the following verses is more likely to be from a **ballad**? Tick (✓) the correct answer.

a

The lamps now glitter down the street;
Faintly sound the falling feet;
And the blue even slowly falls
About the garden trees and walls. ☐

b

The shearers christened him Noisy Ned,
With an alias "Silent Waters",
But never a needless word he said
In the hut or the shearers' quarters. ☐

Student A: Marco's draft

Marco's Year 5 class have to write the first two stanzas of a **ballad**, using Henry Lawson's poem, 'Ballad of the Drover', as a pattern.

To get the feel of a ballad, Marco carefully studied the first four stanzas from Lawson's poem.

1 Across the stony ridges,
Across the rolling plain,
Young Harry Dale, the drover,
Comes riding home again.
And well his stock-horse bears him,
And light of heart is he,
And stoutly his old packhorse
Is trotting by his knee.

2 Up Queensland way with cattle
He's travelled regions vast,
And many months have vanished
Since home-folks saw him last.
He hums a song of someone
He hopes to marry soon;
And hobble-chains and camp-ware
Keep jingling to the tune.

3 Beyond the hazy dado
Against the lower skies
And yon blue line of ranges
The station homestead lies.
And thitherward the drover
Jogs through the lazy noon,
While hobble-chains and camp-ware
Are jingling to a tune.

4 An hour has filled the heavens
With storm-clouds inky black;
At times the lightning trickles
Around the drover's track;
But Harry pushes onward,
His horses' strength he tries,
In hope to reach the river
Before the flood shall rise.

1 Instead of four lines per stanza, Lawson has used eight. Which lines **rhyme** in each stanza? Tick (✓) the correct answer.

a 2 and 4; 5 and 6 ☐

b 1 and 3; 5 and 7 ☐

c 2 and 4; 6 and 8 ☐

2 The **stressed syllables** in these lines from the poem have been underlined. How many syllables are stressed in each one?

a Be-yond the ha-zy da-do ______________________

b A-gainst the low-er skies ______________________

3 Now underline the syllables that should be **stressed** in these lines from the poem.

Hint! Read the lines out loud.

a A-cross the sto-ny ri-dges

b Comes ri-ding home a-gain

c Up Queens-land way with cat-tle

d And hob-ble-chains and camp-ware

4 Highlight the **lines** that are repeated in Lawson's poem.

Writing the first draft

This is Marco's **first attempt** at writing his own **ballad**. Read what he wrote and then answer the questions.

Ballad of the Surfer

Across the embankment,
Across the sand,
There goes Ollie Smith the surfer,
He's going to ride the waves.
He is carrying his longboard,
While looking at the waves.
He can't wait for the thrill
Of riding one home.

When he reaches the water,
It goes around his toes,
And as if by magic,
He forgets all his worries.
He swims through the breakers,
And sings a song,
And he lies on his longboard,
And waits for a wave.

1. A good **ballad** should contain the following features. Tick (✓) the ones that Marco has included.

   a someone's **story** ☐

   b a **regular rhyme pattern** ☐

   c a strong, **regular** beat or **rhythm** ☐

   d interesting **adjectives** (e.g. *strong, tanned*) ☐

   e **descriptive verbs** (e.g. *strides, swoops*) ☐

   f **stanzas** and **lines** that have the **correct spelling** ☐

2. **a** What is the setting for Marco's poem? ______________________

   b Who is the main character in Marco's poem? ______________________

   c Tell what the main character is doing in one sentence. ______________________

   ____

Step-by-step improvement plan

Marco has written only a bare outline of a **ballad**. There are a number of features that he can add to it to turn it into a good, interesting poem. He is going to do some practice exercises to find ways to do this. Help him complete them.

Step 1: Add interesting adjectives

Adjectives give information about nouns. For example: **rough** water, **calm** water.

Not only do adjectives add colour and interest to our writing, but they also help the reader form a vivid mental image of the person, place or thing being written about.

Marco can add colour and interest to his ballad by using good adjectives to describe some of the nouns he has used.

1 Find three **adjectives** in the box to describe each of the nouns below.

tall	joyful	little	tanned	green
crashing	soft	young	rolling	happy
grassed	sloping	white	damp	swelling

a embankment ______ ______ ______

b sand ______ ______ ______

c Ollie Smith ______ ______ ______

d waves ______ ______ ______

e song ______ ______ ______

Step 2: Add descriptive verbs

A **verb** tells **what** happens and **when** it happens. Some verbs are more descriptive than others.

For example: *stride* and *dash* are more descriptive than *walk* and *run*.

Like adjectives, **descriptive verbs** add colour and interest to our writing, as well as allowing the reader to better visualise the action.

1 Circle the most **descriptive verb** in brackets that will add more interest and colour to these lines from Marco's ballad.

a There (goes/walks/strides) Ollie Smith the surfer

b While (looking/gazing/peeping) at the waves

c The water (goes/curls/comes) around his toes

d He (goes/swims/paddles) through the breakers

e He (lies/floats/rests) on his longboard

2 Now think of at least three more **descriptive verbs** that can be used in place of the following words.

a sits ______ ______ ______

b jumps ______ ______ ______

Step 3: Add rhyming words

Rhyming words are words that have a similar end sound.

For example: pl**ain**, ag**ain**; **soon**, **tune**.

For Marco to follow the same rhyme pattern that Henry Lawson has used in 'Ballad of the Drover', he needs to find words that rhyme with *sand, waves, toes* and *song.*

Place the words that **rhyme** on the same page.

paves	along	snows	lows	strong	gong
goes	hand	belong	wrong	craves	bows
fanned	rows	caves	land	planned	long
throng	knaves	tanned	foes	braves	
saves	stand	raves	band	woes	

Words that rhyme with *sand*	Words that rhyme with *waves*	Words that rhyme with *toes*	Words that rhyme with *song*
______	______	______	______
______	______	______	______
______	______	______	______
______	______	______	______
______	______	______	______
______	______	______	______
______	______	______	______

Step 4: Write lines with a strong, regular rhythm

Rhythm is the sense of movement in a poem. The rhythm in Henry Lawson's ballad depends on the regular number of syllables that are stressed in each line.

Example: Across the **stony ridges**,
Across the **rolling plain**

Together with rhyme, rhythm adds to the musicality of the poem.

1. Which line contains the stronger, more regular **rhythm**? Tick (✓) the correct answers.

a	Across the sloping embankment	☐	Across the grassed embankment	☐
b	He is carrying a longboard	☐	Beneath his arm a longboard	☐
c	And now he's reached the water	☐	When he reaches the water	☐
d	The water works its magic	☐	And as if by magic	☐
e	He swims through the breakers	☐	He paddles through the breakers	☐

2. Underline the **adjective** that adds to the **rhythm** of the following line.

And sings a (delightful, happy, short) song

Writing the final draft

This is Marco's **final draft**. He has even added another stanza. Read the comments about his **ballad** on the left, and do the tasks on the right.

Comments

*Using interesting **adjectives** adds colour and interest to the poem and helps the reader form a vivid mental image of the scene being described.*

*Using **descriptive verbs** has a similar effect to using good adjectives. They add interest to the poem and help the reader visualise the action more clearly.*

*Using a definite **rhyme pattern** adds to the musicality of the poem.*

*Writing lines that contain three stressed syllables gives the ballad a strong, regular **rhythm**, while also adding to the musicality of the poem.*

Ballad of the Surfer

Across the grassed embankment,
Across the soft white sand,
Young Ollie Smith the surfer,
Is striding, tall and tanned.
Beneath his arm a longboard,
Before him rolling waves.
They hold for him the promise,
Of thrills that he so craves.

And now he's reached the water,
It curls around his toes.
The water works its magic,
And banishes his woes.
He paddles through the breakers,
And hums a happy song,
And he floats upon his longboard,
Till the right wave comes along.

Then he rises, tall and strong,
Moves to get his balance right,
And he swoops towards the beach
Like a bird that's in full flight.
Then young Ollie Smith the surfer
Heads out to sea once more
To await another wave
To sweep him back towards the shore.

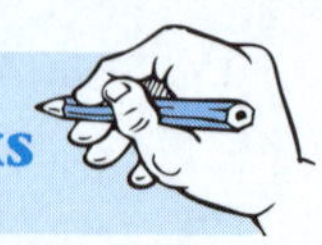

Tasks

1. **Underline** the words that **rhyme**.
2. **Circle** all the **adjectives**.
3. **Underline** the **syllables** that should be stressed in the first two lines.
4. **Circle** five **descriptive verbs**.
5. **Underline** the words that **rhyme**.
6. **Underline** the **syllables** that should be stressed in the last two lines.

Student B: Bianca's draft

Bianca, another Year 5 student, is going to study the last four stanzas of Henry Lawson's poem before writing her **ballad**.

1

The thunder growls a warning
The blue, forked lightnings gleam;
The drover turns his horses
To swim the fatal stream.
But, oh! the flood runs stronger
Than e'er it ran before;
The saddle-horse is failing,
And only half-way o'er!

2

When flashes next the lightning,
The flood's grey breast is blank;
A cattle-dog and packhorse
Are struggling up the bank.
But in the lonely homestead
The girl shall wait in vain—
He'll never pass the stations
In charge of stock again.

3

The faithful dog a moment
Lies panting on the bank,
Then plunges through the current
To where his master sank.
And round and round in circles
He fights with failing strength,
Till, gripped by wilder waters,
He fails and sinks at length.

4

Across the flooded lowlands
And slopes of sodden loam
The packhorse struggles bravely
To take dumb tidings home;
And mud-stained, wet, and weary,
He goes by rock and tree,
With clanging chains and tinware
All sounding eerily.

1. Underline the **syllables** that should be stressed in these lines from the poem.

   The thun-der growls a warn-ing

   The blue, forked light-nings gleam;

   The dro-ver turns his hor-ses

   To swim the fa-tal stream.

2. Which letter has been left out in the words *e'er* and *o'er*? ______________

3. What happens to the drover in these final stanzas of the poem?

Writing the first draft

Bianca is going to tell the story of Annie Tran. This is her **first draft**. Read it and then answer the questions.

Ballad of the Dancer

Annie Tran the dancer
Dances across the floor,
She is steady on her feet
Because she knows the steps so well.
Now she's doing pirouettes,
She's going round and round.
She's doing twirls
While standing on her toes.

She practises for hours and hours
Until her legs are sore
And her body is tired
And her feet are hurting.
But her heart is full of joy
Because she likes to dance.
She would like to dance all day,
It's all she wants to do.

1. Which of these features has Bianca remembered to include in her draft? Tick (✓) the correct answers.

   a telling someone's **story** ☐
   b a **regular rhyme pattern** ☐
   c a strong, **regular** beat or **rhythm** for all lines ☐
   d interesting **adjectives** ☐
   e **descriptive verbs** ☐
   f **stanzas** and **lines** with the correct spelling ☐

2. **a** Where do the events in the **poem** take place?

   ____

   b What is happening in the **poem**?

   ____

   ____

   ____

   ____

   c List three **adjectives** that Bianca has used.

   __________ __________ __________

Step-by-step improvement plan

Bianca has made similar mistakes in her draft to those that Marco made in his. Like Marco, she is going to do some practice exercises to turn her draft into a good, interesting **ballad**. Help her complete them.

Step 1: Add interesting adjectives

While Bianca has used some adjectives, she could include a few more to add further interest and colour to her ballad.

Which **adjectives** from the box could she use to complete each of these lines?

graceful	sure	small	dainty	weary
happy	sore	excellent	young	joyful
certain	perfect	little	pointed	

1. ____________ Annie Tran the dancer
2. Her steps are ____________ and steady
3. Doing ____________ ____________ twirls
4. On the tips of ____________ toes.
5. And ____________ is her body
6. Her feet so very ____________
7. But she has a ____________ heart.

Step 2: Add descriptive verbs

1. Bianca has not used any **descriptive verbs** in her draft. Circle the ones that she could use in place of *dances*.

flits	floats	marches	spins	tramps
stomps	glides	hovers	bounces	rolls

2. Instead of using the word *pirouettes* as a noun, she could change the line to use it as a **descriptive verb**. Fill in the correct form of the word.

   And now she's ____________

3. Circle the **verb** that can best replace *likes* in *Because she likes to dance.*

adores	enjoys	wants	loves	cherishes

4. Find three words that could be used in place of *hurting* in *And her feet are hurting*. Use a thesaurus to help you find suitable **synonyms**.

   ____________ ____________ ____________

Step 3: Add rhyming words

One of the reasons that Bianca's poem lacks the strong rhythm of a ballad is that it does not have a **rhyme pattern**. She needs to make her words rhyme at the ends of lines 2 and 4 and at the ends of lines 6 and 8 in each stanza.

1. Add TWO more words to each of these lists of **rhyming** words.

   a floor—claw, core, door, before, four, sore, jaw, law, ______________ , ______________

   b well—bell, dwell, sell, swell, ______________ , ______________

   c round—bound, found, crowned, ground, ______________ , ______________

   d toes—rose, goes, bows, chose, ______________ , ______________

   e dance—chance, enhance, ______________ , ______________

   f do—blue, flew, glue, who, ______________ , ______________

2. Now choose a word from the lists above to make each pair of lines **rhyme**.

She leaps across the floor
E'en though her feet are ______________

Round and round she ______________
While standing on her toes.

Because all she'd do is dance
If you gave her half a ______________

Step 4: Write lines with a strong, regular rhythm

Another reason Bianca's poem lacks rhythm is that it does not have a regular pattern of **stressed syllables**.

Underline the word in brackets that will give each of these lines the **stronger rhythm**.

1. (Little/Young) Annie Tran the dancer
2. Glides lightly (o'er/across) the floor
3. And now she's (twirling/pirouetting)
4. On the tips of (her/pointed) toes
5. And (weary/weak) is her body
6. (Next/Following) day she's back at training
7. Then she's ready to (start/begin)

Writing the final draft

Bianca has started writing the **final draft** of her **ballad**. Help her complete it, and then look in the answers section to compare what you have written with what Bianca wrote.

Hint! Use Bianca's draft and the practice exercises to help you.

Ballad of the Dancer

Annie Tran the dancer
Dances across the floor,
She is steady on her feet
Because she knows the steps so well.
Now she's doing pirouettes,
She's going round and round.
She's doing twirls
While standing on her toes.
She practises for hours and hours
Until her legs are sore
And her body is tired
And her feet are hurting.
But her heart is full of joy
Because she likes to dance.
She would like to dance all day,
It's all she wants to do.

The Ballad of the Dancer

Young Annie Tran the dancer
Glides lightly o'er the floor.
Her steps ____________________
She's done them all ____________.
And now she's ________________,
Round ______________________
Doing perfect little twirls
On ________________________.
After practising for hours
Her legs can take no more,
And weary __________________
Her feet ____________________
But joyful is her heart
For Annie _________________,
It's all she'd ever do
If _________________________.
Next day she's back at training.
She glides onto the floor,
Her legs no longer weary,
Her feet no longer ___________.
She starts by doing warm-ups,
Then she's ready to __________,
There's a competition soon
That she'd really like to _________!

Your turn

Write two to three stanzas of a **ballad** on one of the following. Use your own paper for this activity.

Writing Checklist Make sure your ballad: ✓

- tells someone's **story**. ☐
- has a **regular rhyme pattern**. ☐
- has a strong, **regular** beat or **rhythm**. ☐
- contains interesting **adjectives**. ☐
- contains **descriptive verbs**. ☐
- is divided into **stanzas** and **lines** that have the **correct spelling**. ☐

Tip Use **Marco's final draft** on page 78 and **Bianca's final draft** on page 83 to help you write your ballad.

Go to WORD BANK pages 135–136 for useful vocabulary

1. Write a ballad about a boy or girl who loves doing something, like skateboarding, acting, bike riding, cooking or drawing.

   Use Marco and Bianca's ballads as models.

2. Write the first three stanzas of a ballad based on the following poem by Henry Lawson. Instead of Andy taking cattle across the Queensland border, you could write about a girl or boy going away on a school camp or a sports tour.

   Notice that this poem has only four lines to a stanza and the rhyme pattern is a-b-a-b, with lines 2 and 4 often ending with the same word.

Our Andy's gone with cattle now—
Our hearts are out of order—
With drought he's gone to battle now
Across the Queensland border.

He's left us in dejection now;
Our thoughts with him are roving;
It's dull on this selection now,
Since Andy went a-droving.

Who now shall wear the cheerful face
In times when things are slackest?
And who shall whistle round the place
When fortune frowns her blackest?

Unit 8 Discussions

Looking at discussions

A **discussion** looks at both sides of an argument.

The main **purpose** of a discussion is to provide a **balanced** view of the issue that is fair to both sides.

A **discussion** should have:

- an **opening statement** that introduces the issue and previews the main arguments.
- **arguments for**, with supporting evidence.
- **arguments against**, with supporting evidence.
- a **conclusion** that refers back briefly to the arguments and then comes to a conclusion on one side or the other; sometimes it makes a recommendation.

1 Which of these texts is more likely to be the opening statement of a **discussion**? Tick (✓) the correct answer.

a Many students complain about having to wear a uniform to school, but I believe it's a good thing. ☐

b Many students complain about having to wear a uniform to school. While wearing a uniform has many advantages, it also has some drawbacks. ☐

2 Which of these sentences is more likely to be the **concluding statement** of a discussion? Tick (✓) the correct answer.

a Rather than banning all pets from apartments, perhaps only large or noisy ones, like dogs, should be banned. ☐

b I am certain that the arguments I have presented will convince you that all pets should be banned from apartments, no matter how big or small, noisy or quiet they are. ☐

Student A: Ashley's draft

Ashley's Year 5 class have been discussing whether it would be better to use fans rather than air conditioners to cool the classrooms during the hot summer months.

Now they have to present their views as a written **discussion**.

Before she starts writing, Ashley jots down words and phrases to remind her of the arguments she would like to make for and against using fans instead of air conditioners in summer.

> Fans use less electricity—can't cool classroom on hottest days—good for environment—blow papers on desks away—cheaper to run—cost less—only have two or three speeds—air conditioners can be adjusted easily to different temperatures—can open windows—fresh air—perhaps better for our health—fans only help those sitting close to them—air conditioners cool everyone in the room

1. Help Ashley organise her ideas by writing them in the correct column.

Using fans rather than air conditioners to cool our classrooms

Advantages	**Disadvantages**
a	a
b	b
c	c
d	d

2. Which do you think is the **strongest argument** for using fans?

Writing the first draft

This is Ashley's **first draft**. Read what she wrote and then answer the questions.

Are fans better than air conditioners?

Are fans better than air conditioners?

They are better because they use less electricity. That is good for the environment. They are cheaper to run than air conditioners because they don't use as much electricity. That is a good thing. They cost less than air conditioners. That is good. When you use fans you can keep the windows open. Fresh air is good for students. Fans do not work well on very hot days. That's when we need air conditioners. Fans blow papers off desks. Students and teachers find this annoying. Air conditioners don't blow papers away.

I think that fans are good sometimes and air conditioners are good at other times.

1 A good **discussion** should contain the following features. Tick (✓) the ones that Ashley has used.

- **a** an interesting **opening statement** that **introduces** the **issue** and **previews** the **main arguments** ☐
- **b** **arguments for** the idea ☐
- **c** **arguments against** the idea ☐
- **d** strong **supporting evidence** for **arguments** ☐
- **e** a **conclusion** that refers briefly to the arguments and provides a **recommendation** ☐
- **f** **connectives** to **link ideas** and make the **writing flow** (e.g. *In the first place, On the other hand, However*) ☐
- **g** **synonyms** for words like *good* and *bad* to **add interest** and **variety** to the text ☐
- **h** **present-tense verbs** (e.g. *is, use*) ☐
- **i** **sentences** with **correct spelling** and **punctuation** ☐

One of the things that Ashley has remembered to do in her draft is to use the **present tense** throughout.

2 Find five **present-tense verbs** in the draft and underline them.

Step-by-step improvement plan

While Ashley has got the basic structure of a **discussion** right, she has not provided strong **supporting evidence** for her arguments. Her writing also lacks fluency. Ashley is going to do some practice exercises to find ideas on how she can improve her draft. Help her complete them.

Step 1: Start with a good opening statement

The **opening statement** is the introduction to the discussion. It needs to draw the reader in by stating the issue to be discussed in an interesting way.

Put these phrases and clauses together to construct a more interesting **opening** for Ashley's discussion.

after running around	but I enjoy the feeling of walking into an air conditioned classroom	fans or air conditioners
which is more beneficial		I am a big fan of fans
the question is	on a hot summer's day	on the playground

Step 2: Add variety with synonyms

Synonyms are words that have similar meanings. For example: *good* and *fine*.

Using synonyms for words that are repeated often in a text adds variety and interest.

1. The words in the box are **synonyms** for either *advantages* or *disadvantages*. Place them in the correct column.

drawbacks	problems	merits	bonuses	positives	strengths
pluses	pros	downsides	cons	weaknesses	benefits
blessings	negatives	minuses	faults		

Hint! Some of these need to be used together. For example: *pluses* and *minuses*. You would not use *pluses* and then, for example, *drawbacks* in the next clause or sentence.

Advantages	Disadvantages

2. Choose a word from the list above to complete each of these sentences. Use a different word each time.

   a. One of the ______________ of using fans is that they are cheaper to run.

   b. One of the ______________ of having only fans in a classroom is that they do not cool the air on a very hot day.

   c. On the whole, I think the ______________ of using mainly fans outweigh the ______________.

Step 3: Link ideas with connectives

In Unit 4 you learnt that **connectives** can be adverbs, adverbial phrases or conjunctions. We use them to link paragraphs, sentences and parts of sentences so that our writing flows.

Fill in **connectives** from the box to make this version of Ashley's draft read more fluently. Use each connective once. The first one has been done for you.

as	on the other hand	furthermore	all in all	because
in addition	also	and	on the one hand	

On the one hand, fans are better for the environment ______________ they use less electricity. They are ______________ cheaper to run ______________ cost less than air conditioners.

____________________, we can still get fresh air into the classrooms when we use fans ______________ we can keep the windows open.

____________________________, fans do not work well on very hot days. That's when we need air conditioners.

____________________, fans blow papers off desks, which is something air conditioners don't do.

____________________, I think that fans are good sometimes and air conditioners are good at other times.

Step 4: End with a good conclusion

The **conclusion** is the last paragraph. It should refer briefly to the arguments and provide a recommendation.

Help Ashley write a good **conclusion** for her discussion by filling in the gaps.

While there is a strong case for using fans to cool our classrooms, I believe that

____

____

Perhaps ____

____

____

Writing the final draft

This is Ashley's **final draft**. Read the comments about her **discussion** on the left, and do the tasks on the right.

Comments | **Tasks**

Should we use fans or air conditioners to cool our classrooms?

Introducing the issue and previewing the main arguments in the ***opening statement*** *gives the reader a clear picture of what is to follow.*

I am a big fan of fans, but I also enjoy the feeling of walking into an air-conditioned classroom after running around on the playground on a hot summer's day. The question is, which is more beneficial—fans, or air conditioners?

1. Underline the **synonym** of better.

Using ***connectives*** *to link ideas makes the writing flow.*

Providing ***supporting evidence*** *adds strength to the* ***arguments****.*

Firstly, fans are definitely better for the environment because they use less electricity than air conditioners. Electricity is mainly made by burning coal, and as scientists keep warning us, this is one of the causes of global warming. So the less electricity we use, the better it is for the environment.

2. Underline the sentence that gives **evidence** to support the main argument.

Secondly, fans are cheaper to run. They also cost less. By using fans rather than air conditioners, the school will save money, which can be spent on projects such as upgrading equipment.

3. Underline the sentence that expresses the **main argument**.

Using ***synonyms*** *for words that have appeared before adds variety and interest.*

Another benefit of using fans is that they do their job even if the windows are open. This allows fresh air to enter the classrooms, creating a healthy environment for students to work in.

4. Circle two **adjectives**.

Looking at both sides of the issue provides a ***balanced view****.*

However, there are disadvantages to using only fans. In the first place, they do not cool the air on very hot days. Air conditioners, on the other hand, can be adjusted easily to different temperatures so that even on the hottest day, they cool everyone in the room.

5. Circle the word that indicates a change in the writer's **point of view**.

In addition, fans often blow papers off desks, which teachers and students find annoying. This is not a problem with air conditioners.

6. Underline the **connective**.

Including a ***recommendation*** *in the concluding paragraph shows that the writer has thought carefully about the issue.*

While there is a strong case for using fans to cool our classrooms, I believe that we also need air conditioners. Perhaps we can use air conditioners on very hot days and fans the rest of the time.

7. Underline the writer's **recommendation**.

Student B: Ravi's draft

Ravi is in a different Year 5 class. They have been discussing the pros and cons of the principal's plan to divide the playground into sections, with each year group having their own section to play in at recess and lunchtime. The principal has asked the students in Ravi's class to write a **discussion** in which they put forward the benefits and drawbacks of this idea.

Before expressing his views on the subject, Ravi jots down some arguments he could use.

> Will keep younger ones safe—older students can be rough—some students have friends in other year groups—students won't get to know each other—help students bond with others in their year—might be difficult to keep students apart—don't always obey rules—hard for teachers to manage—need more teachers on playground duty—more work for teachers—some areas of the playground more interesting than others—who gets the good areas?—older students might boss younger ones

1 Ravi's **arguments** for and against the principal's idea are a bit muddled. Sort them out and write them under the following headings.

Benefits	**Drawbacks**
a ______________________ ______________________	a ______________________ ______________________
b ______________________ ______________________	b ______________________ ______________________
c ______________________ ______________________	c ______________________ ______________________
d ______________________ ______________________	d ______________________ ______________________
e ______________________ ______________________	e ______________________ ______________________

2 Which do you think is the **strongest argument** for keeping the year groups separate at recess and lunch break?

____

____

Writing the first draft

This is Ravi's **first draft**. Read it and then answer the questions.

> Ms Iannella wants to divide the playground into sections so each year group has its own area to play in. Is this good or bad?
>
> It will stop younger students getting hurt. The older students can sometimes be quite rough. So dividing up the playground would be a good thing.
>
> It will encourage students to make friends with people of their own age. There will be no younger or older ones to play with. That is good.
>
> It will be bad because students with friends in different groups won't be able to play with each other.
>
> It will be hard for teachers to keep everyone apart. I wonder if the teachers even know which group everyone belongs to.
>
> It will be bad if we always have to play in the same area. Some of us will never get to play on the equipment.
>
> Ms Iannella's plan has some good points and some bad points.

1 Which of these things has Ravi remembered to include in his draft? Tick (✓) the correct answers.

- **a** an interesting **opening statement** that **introduces** the **issue** and **previews** the **main arguments** ☐
- **b** **arguments for** the idea ☐
- **c** **arguments against** the idea ☐
- **d** strong **evidence** to support his **arguments** ☐
- **e** a **recommendation** in his **conclusion** ☐

2 Which of these **language features** has Ravi used in his draft?

- **a** **connectives** to **link ideas** ☐
- **b** **synonyms** for words like *good* and *bad* to **add interest** and **variety** to the text ☐
- **c** **present-tense verbs** (e.g. *is, use*) ☐

Step-by-step improvement plan

While Ravi has done some things well in his draft, there is room for improvement. He is going to do some practice exercises to find ways to make his **discussion** more interesting for the principal to read. Help him complete them.

Step 1: Start with a good opening statement

1. Although Ravi has stated the issue in his **opening statement**, his opening paragraph could be stronger. Help Ravi write a more interesting opening statement for his discussion.

   Complete this paragraph.

   Mrs Iannella, our principal, wants to divide ______________________________

   ____

   ____

   ____

   While the idea has many advantages, it also ______________________________

   ____

   ____

Step 2: Add variety with synonyms

Ravi's draft lacks variety because he has used the words *good* and *bad* too often to describe the advantages and disadvantages of Ms Iannella's plan.

Complete these sentences that contain **synonyms** for *advantages* and *disadvantages* and then underline the synonym in each sentence.

1. One of the benefits of giving each group their own area to play in is that

   ____

   ____

2. While there are positives to the idea, ______________________________

   ____

   ____

3. One of the drawbacks of separating the year groups at recess and lunch break is that

   ____

   ____

4. One of the problems for the teachers is that ______________________________

   ____

   ____

5. A definite plus for some groups is that ______________________________

   ____

   ____

Step 3: Link ideas with connectives

Ravi's writing does not flow because he has not used connectives to link his ideas. Complete this passage with **connectives** from the box. Use each connective once. The first one has been done for you.

Hint! Remember that the passage needs to make sense.

and	on the positive side	in addition	as	a further problem	also

On the positive side, Ms Iannella's plan will keep the younger students safe. Some of the older students like to play rough games, ____________ if the little ones get in the way, they sometimes get injured.

Another plus is that students will have to play with people in their own year group ____________ they will no longer be able to play with those who are younger or older than themselves. This could create stronger bonds between students in the same group.

One of the negatives is that students with friends in different groups won't be able to play with each other. This might make them unhappy.

It will ____________ be hard for teachers to keep everyone apart. ________________, not all the teachers know which group some of the students belong to.

________________________ is that if we always have to play in the same area, some of us will never get to play on the equipment.

Step 4: End with a good conclusion

Ravi's conclusion is not strong enough and does not contain a **recommendation**.

1. Rearrange the sentences below to form a stronger, more interesting **conclusion** for Ravi's discussion by numbering them in the correct order.

a This would make it fair for everyone. ☐

b I also think that the groups should be rotated so that each group gets to play in a different section of the playground every day. ☐

c For Ms Iannella's plan to work, I believe that the Kindergarten and Year 1 and 2 classes should form one group, the Year 3 and 4s another group, and the Year 5 and 6s the third group. ☐

2. Underline Ravi's recommendations.

Writing the final draft

Ravi has started writing the **final draft** of his **discussion**. Help him complete it by filling in the missing sections, and then look in the answers section to compare what you have written with what Ravi wrote.

Hint! Look at Ravi's notes and the practice exercises for ideas.

(Write a good opening statement for Ravi's discussion.)

....

....

....

....

....

On the positive side, giving the younger students their own area to play in

(Continue this paragraph by outlining the positives.)

....

....

....

....

....

Another advantage of keeping the groups apart is that students in the same year group will have to play together. Often older students like to play with the younger ones because they can boss them around.

However, I feel that there are drawbacks to Ms Iannella's plan.

(Write a paragraph about the problem of having friends in other year groups.)

....

....

....

....

....

(Write a paragraph about some sections of the playground being more interesting to play in.)

....

....

(Write a paragraph about the difficulties teachers on playground duty might have.)

For Ms Iannella's plan to work, I believe that the Kindergarten and Year 1 and 2 classes should form one group, the Year 3 and 4s another group, and the Year 5 and 6s the third group. I also think that the groups should be rotated around the playground, so that each group gets to experience a different section of the playground every day. This would ensure that everyone gets a fair deal.

Your turn

Write a **discussion** of one to two pages on one of the following. Use your own paper for this activity.

Writing Checklist Make sure your discussion includes: ✓

- an interesting **opening statement** that **introduces** the **issue** and **previews** the **main arguments**. ☐
- **arguments for** and **against** with **supporting evidence**. ☐
- a **conclusion** that refers briefly to the **arguments** and provides a **recommendation**. ☐
- **connectives** to **link ideas**. ☐
- **synonyms** for words like *good* and *bad* to **add interest** and **variety**. ☐
- **present-tense** verbs. ☐

Tip Use **Ashley's final draft** on page 90 and **Ravi's final draft** on page 95 to help you write your dicussions.

Go to WORD BANK page 136 for useful vocabulary

1. Discuss the advantages and disadvantages of school excursions.
2. Should teachers stop giving homework?

Unit 9 Explanations

Looking at explanations

An **explanation** is an informative text. Its main **purpose** is to explain **why** something happens or **how** it works.

An explanation should:

- have an **opening statement** that **introduces** the topic and **describes** or **identifies** the phenomenon.
- be divided into a **series of paragraphs** that give a sequenced explanation of how the phenomenon works or why it happens.
- end with a **conclusion** that either sums up the explanation or ties it up in some other way.

Hint! Diagrams are often used to support the text.

1 Which of these are most likely to be the titles of **explanation** texts? Tick (✓) the correct answers.

- a What causes a tsunami? ☐
- b A day in the life of a zookeeper ☐
- c How a snake moves along the ground ☐
- d Why snakes have scales ☐
- e The pros and cons of keeping snakes as pets ☐

2 Which of these sentences might appear in the opening paragraph of an **explanation** on how muscles work? Tick (✓) the correct answer.

- a He flexed his muscles to show everyone how strong he was. ☐
- b A muscle is a bundle of fibrous tissue in a human or animal's body. ☐
- c Rubbing ointment into sore muscles can sometimes relieve the stiffness. ☐

3 Which of these sentences is more likely to be part of an **explanation**? Tick (✓) the correct answer.

A Electricity travels from the power plant to your home through a circuit. ☐

B Electricity is definitely the world's most important invention. ☐

Student A: Matthew's draft

Matthew's Year 5 class have been discussing ways to stay healthy.
To gain a better understanding of the body and how it works, they have to choose one of the body's processes and write an **explanation** of how it works. Matthew is going to write about the heart.

First Matthew studied this poster.

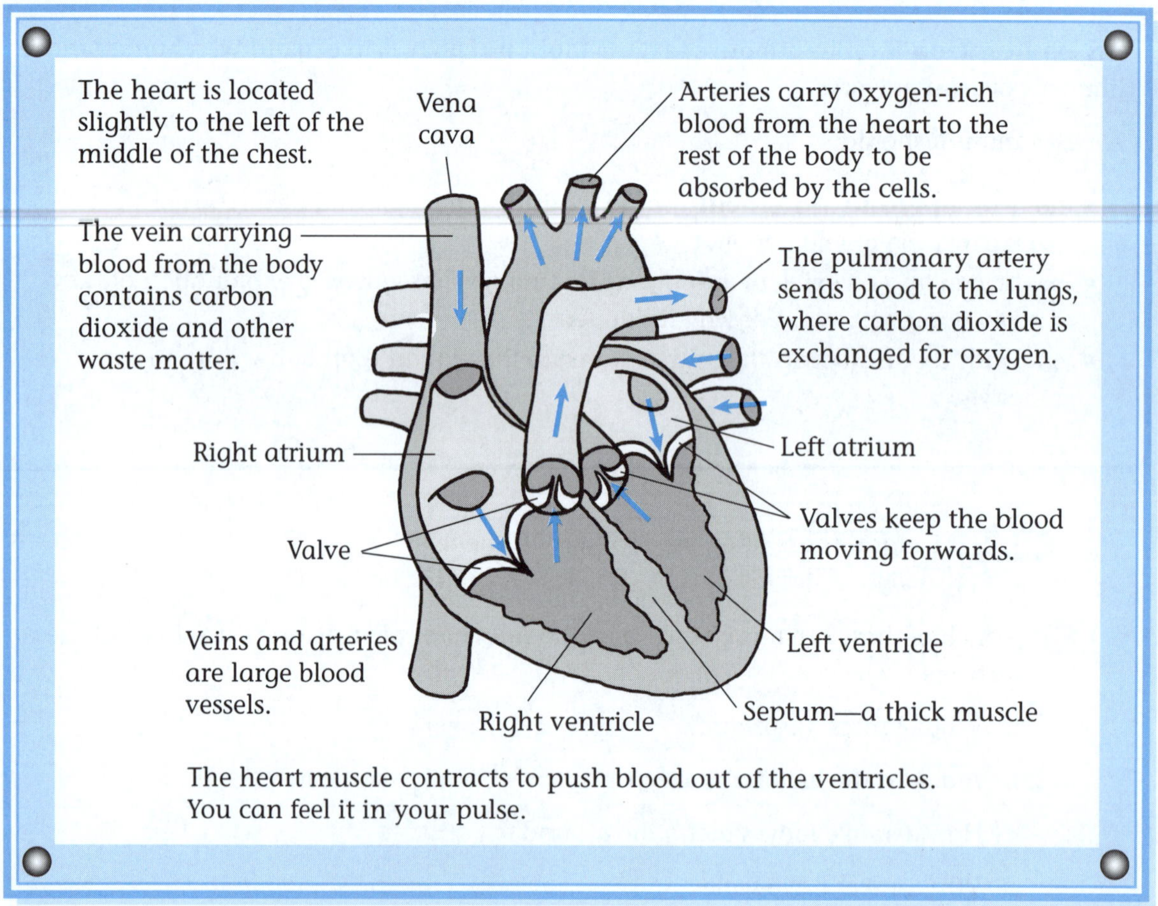

How much do you already know about the heart?

1. What does a doctor use to listen to your heart? ______________________

2. How can you measure the number of times your heart beats in a minute?

____

3. What is the image of a heart often used to symbolise? ____________

4. A kind person is often said to have a heart of ____________ .

5. Which of these is a doctor likely to recommend as a way of keeping your heart healthy? Tick (✓) the correct answer.

   a read ☐

   b play computer games ☐

   c exercise ☐

Writing the first draft

After studying the poster, Matthew was ready to write the **first draft**. Read what he wrote and then answer the questions.

How the heart works

The heart is in the chest. It is a muscle. It pumps blood around the body.

It has four parts called chambers. There is a muscle down the middle. A tube brings blood from the body to the top right chamber. This blood has waste in it. The blood goes into the bottom right chamber. It goes through another tube to the lungs. The lungs clean the blood. They give it oxygen. The blood goes back to the heart in another tube. It goes into the top left chamber. Then it goes into the bottom left chamber. It leaves the heart through another tube and takes the oxygen to all parts of the body.

1. A good **explanation** should contain the following features. Tick (✓) the ones Matthew has used.

   a. an **opening paragraph** that introduces the topic with a **general statement** that **describes** or **identifies** the phenomenon. ☐

   b. a **sequenced explanation** of **how** the phenomenon works or **why** it happens. ☐

   c. a **conclusion** that either **sums up** the **explanation** or **ties it up** in some other way. ☐

   d. **present-tense verbs** (e.g. *is*, *has* or *goes*). ☐

   e. **passive voice** (e.g. *waste is removed from the blood*). ☐

   f. **technical** or **scientific language** (e.g. *atrium*, *ventricle*). ☐

   g. **paragraphs** that make the **explanation easier to understand**. ☐

   h. **sentences** with **correct spelling** and **punctuation**. ☐

2. Although Matthew hasn't expressed the different stages of the process in separate paragraphs, he has **sequenced** them in a logical way. Answer the questions below in full sentences.

   a. What happens to the blood in the lungs?

   ____

   ____

   b. Where does the blood go after it leaves the lungs?

   ____

   ____

   c. Where does the blood go after it leaves the bottom-left chamber?

   ____

   ____

Step-by-step improvement plan

Matthew has a good understanding of the way the heart works. Now he has to work on presenting his information in a more structured and interesting manner. He is going to do some practice exercises to find ways to do this. Help him complete them.

Step 1: Start with a good introduction

The **introduction** is the first paragraph of the explanation. It should give the reader a brief overview of the phenomenon or process to be explained by stating what it is and what it does.

Matthew could make his **introduction** more interesting by using better sentences that contain a bit more information; for example, by telling the reader that the process whereby blood is pumped around the body is called *circulation*.

Complete the paragraph.

The heart is ______________________________ that is located ______________________________

____

It is responsible for ____

____

This process ____

Step 2: Use the passive voice

Verbs are either **active** or **passive**.

When verbs are active, the person or thing doing the action is the subject of the sentence.
For example: **The heart** pumps blood around the body.

When verbs are passive, the person or thing having the action done to them is the subject of the sentence.
For example: **Blood** is pumped around the body by the heart.

We use the passive voice when we want to emphasise the process or action rather than the doer of the action, especially when people are involved.

Hint! It is important not to overuse the passive voice as it can make the writing sound clumsy.

1 Which of these sentences is in the **passive voice**? Tick (✓) the correct answer.

- **a** A machine recorded my heart rate. ☐
- **b** The fastest heart rate was recorded by Patient B. ☐
- **c** The heart muscle is strengthened by exercise. ☐
- **d** Exercise strengthens the heart muscle. ☐

2 Now write these sentences in the **passive voice**.

a The lungs remove the waste from the blood.

Waste is ______________________________

b The blood carries the oxygen to all parts of the body.

The oxygen is ______________________________

Step 3: Use technical or scientific language

Scientific subjects like the heart and the circulatory system have their own vocabulary to name the different parts and processes (e.g. *atrium*, *ventricle*). Using these **scientific terms** in an explanation gives the text a greater sense of authority because it allows us to talk precisely about the topic. Not using these terms suggests a lack of knowledge.

Matthew has not used many scientific terms in his explanation, so he has looked at the poster again to see which words or terms he can replace or add to his draft.

1 Which **scientific term** can Matthew use in place of the following?

a top-left chamber ____________

b bottom-right chamber ____________

c the muscle down the middle ____________

d the waste matter that the blood contains ____________

e the tubes that carry blood to the heart ____________

2 Make a sentence with one of the terms above.

____

____

Step 4: Add a conclusion to tie up the explanation

The **conclusion** is the final paragraph of the explanation. It should tie up the explanation in an interesting way. Remember—an explanation is a formal, factual text, so the conclusion should not end with a personal opinion or exclamation.

Matthew's explanation ends rather abruptly, so he has added this paragraph about how we can measure the number of times our hearts beat.

> You can tell when your heart contracts to push blood out of the ventricles by feeling the pulse on the side of your neck or the inside of your wrist. When you are resting, your pulse will beat around 70 to 100 times a minute.

Help Matthew choose a final sentence for his **explanation**. Tick (✓) the correct answer.

1 Isn't the heart amazing? ☐

2 During that time the heart will have pumped blood to every cell in the body. ☐

Writing the final draft

This is Matthew's **final draft**. Read the comments about his **explanation** on the left, and do the tasks on the right.

Comments

Starting with a brief **overview** *of the topic prepares the reader for what is to come.*

Using **scientific** *vocabulary gives the writing a sense of authority.*

Sequencing *the stages of the process in a logical manner helps the reader make sense of the text.*

Dividing the text into **paragraphs** *makes it easier to understand.*

Using the **passive voice** *focuses attention on the action rather than the doer of the action.*

Explaining *how we can feel our heart beat is a good way of tying up the explanation.*

How the heart works

The heart is a muscle that is located slightly to the left of the middle of the chest. It is responsible for sending blood around the body. This movement of blood around the body is called circulation.

The heart is divided into four parts, or chambers. The top chambers are the right and left atria, and the bottom chambers are the right and left ventricles. The left and right sides of the heart are divided by a thick muscle called the septum.

Blood carrying carbon dioxide and other waste matter from the body enters the right atrium, from where it passes into the right ventricle. When the heart muscle contracts, the blood is pumped from the right ventricle to the lungs, where the carbon dioxide is exchanged for oxygen.

This oxygen-rich blood then flows to the left atrium and passes into the left ventricle. From here it is pumped to the body's cells, where the oxygen is exchanged for carbon dioxide and other waste matter. The blood containing this waste matter flows back to the right atrium and the process starts all over again.

Blood enters and leaves the heart through tubes called blood vessels. The blood vessels that carry blood to the heart are called veins, and those that carry blood away from the heart are called arteries. The flow of blood through the heart is controlled by valves that keep it moving forwards.

You can tell when your heart contracts to push blood out of the ventricles by feeling the pulse on the side of your neck or the inside of your wrist. When you are resting, your pulse will beat around 70 to 100 times a minute. During that time the heart will have pumped blood to every cell in the body.

Tasks

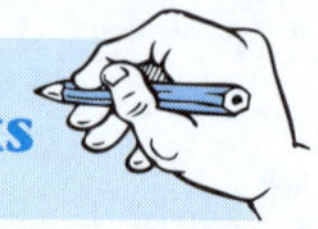

1. **Underline** the **scientific words** that are specific to the heart.
2. **Underline** the word that is **opposite** in meaning to *expands*.
3. **Circle** three **adjectives**.
4. **Underline** the sentence that has been written in the **passive voice**.
5. **Underline** the **concluding statement**.

Student B: Frieda's draft

Frieda, another Year 5 student, is going to write an **explanation** entitled *How our body digests food.*

She starts by studying the information on this poster.

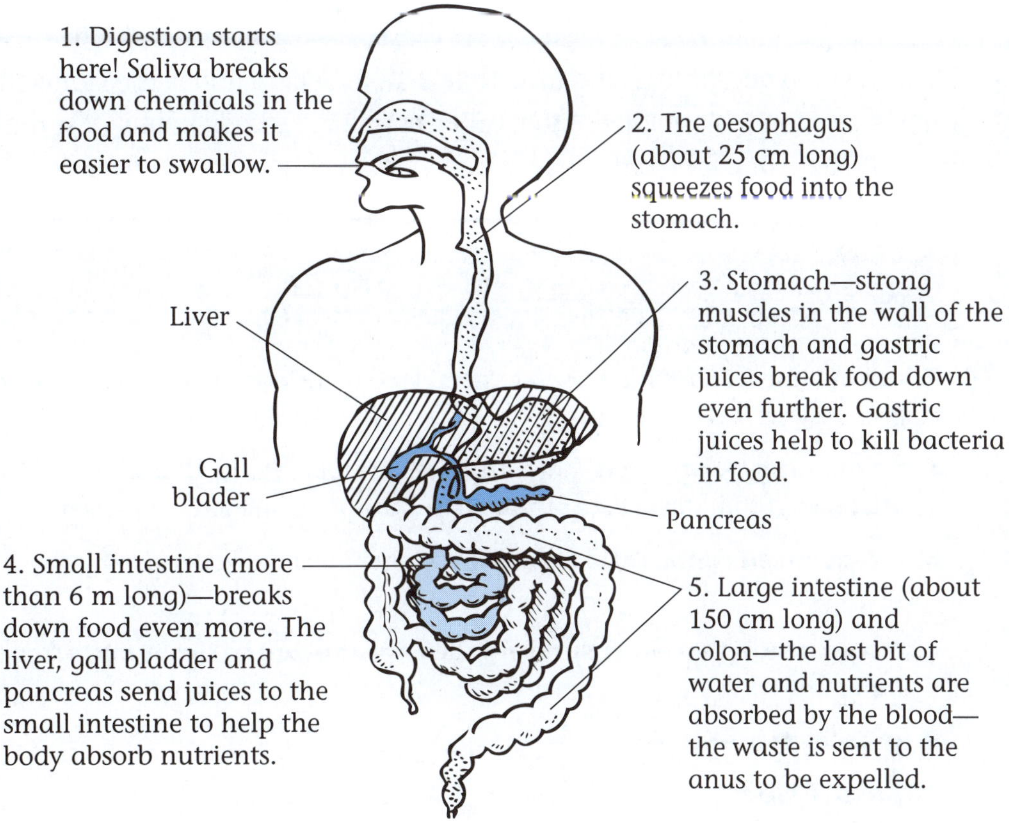

During digestion your body absorbs nutrients such as vitamins, minerals, proteins, carbohydrates and fats from your food. It takes about 33 hours from the time you eat until the waste is expelled, sometimes longer for adults.

Answer the following questions.

1. Where in the body does the digestive process start? ________________

2. How much do you know about nutrition? List five nutrients that our bodies get from the food we eat. ________________

____

3. Which of these foods contains Vitamin C? Tick (✓) the correct answer.

   a sugar ☐ **b** oranges ☐ **c** chips ☐

4. Which food contains the most protein? Tick (✓) the correct answer.

   a eggs ☐ **b** potatoes ☐ **c** chocolates ☐

Writing the first draft

This is Frieda's **first draft**. Read it and then answer the questions.

How our body digests food

Food gives us energy. This happens during digestion. This is how it happens.

First we put the food in our mouths. Then we swallow it and it goes into the stomach, which looks like a sack. Juices in the stomach help break the food down.

Next the food goes into a long tube that is all folded up under the stomach. This tube is very long. More juices from other parts of the body help digest the food here and get out all the nutrients. What is left over goes into another tube, where the water and minerals pass into the bloodstream. Then only waste is left and our bodies get rid of it.

1 Which of these features has Frieda remembered to include in her draft? Tick (✓) the correct answers.

- **a** an **opening paragraph** that introduces the topic with a **general statement** that **describes** or **identifies** the phenomenon ☐
- **b** a **sequenced explanation** of **how** the phenomenon works or **why** it happens ☐
- **c** a **conclusion** that either **sums up** the **explanation** or **ties it up** in some other way ☐
- **d** **present-tense verbs** ☐
- **e** **passive voice** ☐
- **f** **technical** or **scientific language** ☐
- **g** **paragraphs** that make the **explanation easier to understand** ☐
- **h** **sentences** with correct **spelling** and **punctuation** ☐

2 Frieda has left out some important information in her draft. Look at the poster again and then answer the following questions in full sentences.

a What happens to food in our mouths that makes it easier to swallow?

____

____

b What part do the muscles in the walls of the stomach play in the digestive process?

____

____

____

Step-by-step improvement plan

Frieda's **explanation** is fairly easy to follow because she has described the digestive process in a logical way. However, there are a number of important features that are missing from her draft. Frieda is going to do some practice exercises to find ways to improve her draft. Help her complete them.

Step 1: Start with a good introduction

Frieda's opening paragraph does not provide the reader with enough information. She needs to expand the first two sentences so that they contain more detail.

1. Put the words on the notes together to form a good **opening sentence**.

the nutrients and energy | we eat | they need | the food | our bodies get | from

____

____

2. Now put the words on these notes together to complete the **opening paragraph**.

these nutrients | the process | is called digestion | whereby | in our bodies | from the food | are extracted

____

____

Step 2: Use the passive voice

Writing two or three sentences in the passive voice will place the focus on certain digestive processes rather than on what causes the processes to happen.

Write these sentences in the **passive voice**. Start with the underlined words in each case.

1. Strong muscles in the wall of the stomach break the food down even further.

____

2. The blood absorbs any water and minerals that remain in the food.

____

Step 3: Use technical or scientific language

1. Like Matthew's first draft, Frieda's sounds casual and uninformed because she has not used enough scientific terms that are specific to digestion. Help her find the correct **scientific term** for the underlined words in these sentences.

   a The food passes into the throat, from where it is slowly squeezed through a tube into the stomach. ________________

   b The food passes into a long tube that is folded into the area beneath the stomach.

   ____

2. Now make your own sentences with the following words. Use the poster to help you.

   a liver ________________

   b large intestine ________________

   c colon ________________

Step 4: Add a conclusion to tie up the explanation

Frieda has jotted down some words and phrases that she could use to tie up her **explanation**.

1. Help her make them into sentences.

   For example: *finally—remaining water, minerals—absorbed into bloodstream.*

   Finally, the water and minerals that remain in the food are absorbed into the bloodstream.

Hint! Look at the poster if you need help!

   a *what remains—through colon—to anus—expelled*

   ____

   ____

   b *Time—enters mouth—expelled—about 33 hours (child)—sometimes longer (adult)*

   ____

   ____

2. Now put the sentences together to form the final paragraph of the **explanation**.

Writing the final draft

Frieda has started writing the **final draft** of her **procedure**. Help her complete it, and then look in the answers section to compare what you have written with what Frieda wrote.

Hint! Look at the poster and the practice exercises for ideas.

How our body digests food

Our bodies get the nutrients and energy they need from the food we eat. The process whereby these nutrients are extracted from the food in our bodies is called digestion.

(Write a paragraph explaining what happens to the food in the mouth.)

From the mouth, the food passes into the throat, from where it is slowly squeezed through the oesophagus (e-SOF-a-guss) into the stomach. Here it is broken down even further by strong muscles in the walls of the stomach. Gastric juices produced in the walls of the stomach help break the food down, as well as killing any bacteria the food might contain.

Once the food in the stomach is in a liquid state, it passes into the small intestine, a long tube that is folded into the area beneath the stomach. Laid out straight, the small intestine would measure almost seven metres.

(Write a paragraph explaining what happens to the food in the small intestine.)

By the end of its stay in the small intestine, the food is very thin and watery. Nutrients can now pass easily into the bloodstream to be carried to the liver for further processing. What is left in the small intestine moves into the large intestine.

(Write the final paragraph.)

Your turn

Write an **explanation** of one to two pages on one of the following. Use your own paper for this activity.

Writing Checklist Make sure your explanation contains: ✓

- an **opening paragraph** that introduces the topic with a **general statement** that **describes** or **identifies** the phenomenon. ☐
- a **sequenced explanation** of **how** the phenomenon works or **why** it happens. ☐
- a **conclusion** that either **sums up** the **explanation** or **ties it up** in some other way. ☐
- **present-tense verbs**. ☐
- some sentences in the **passive voice**. ☐
- **technical** or **scientific language**. ☐
- **paragraphs** that make the **explanation easier to understand**. ☐
- **sentences** with **correct spelling** and **punctuation**. ☐

Tip Use **Matthew's final draft** on page 102 and **Frieda's final draft** on page 107 to help you write your explanation.

Go to WORD BANK page 136 for useful vocabulary

Write an explanation that describes how one of these processes works.

a respiratory system

b nervous system

c skeletal system

Use Matthew's and Frieda's explanations as models.

Unit 10 Book reviews

Looking at reviews

A **review** examines and gives personal judgements on things such as books, films, plays, concerts, exhibitions and products.

In this unit we will be focusing on book reviews.

A **book review** should have:

- an **introduction** that names the author, genre and title of the book, and that includes a sentence that briefly says what the book is about and perhaps what the reviewer's overall opinion of the book is.
- a **series of paragraphs** that give more detail and opinions about the plot, characters and themes, without revealing the ending.
- a **conclusion** that contains a personal judgement or evaluation of the book and provides a recommendation.

Hint! While all reviews have a similar structure, details such as *name of author* will change to suit the subject being written about.

For example: if a film is being reviewed, it will be *name of director*.

1 Which of the following is the **opening sentence** of a book review? Tick (✓) the correct answer.

a *Frozen* is a 3D computer-animated musical fantasy comedy. ☐

b The *Spitfire 600* is the latest model in the *Hotspurs* range. ☐

c *The Iron Man* is a science fiction novel by Ted Hughes. ☐

2 Which of these sentences expresses an **opinion** about the book, *Onion Tears*? Tick (✓) the correct answer.

a The book is about the difficulties a young girl experiences in a strange environment. ☐

b This is a beautifully written book about a young refugee girl. ☐

c The author of the book, *Onion Tears*, is Diana Kidd. ☐

Student A: Sasha's draft

Sasha's Year 5 class were given two weeks to read a novel. They had to make notes about the novel as they read, and then write a **review** of it afterwards.

Sasha read *Where the Mountain Meets the Moon* by Grace Lin. These are the notes she made in her journal.

Plot: young girl —lives in Valley of Fruitless Mountain—everyone poor—father tells girl stories about Old Man of the Moon —girl sets off to find him—wants to change family's fortune

Characters: Main—Minli, Ma, Ba, Dragon. Other—Goldfish Man, Goldfish, Buffalo Boy, Magistrate Tiger, King of the City of Bright Moonlight, A-Fu, Da-Fu, Old Man of the Moon

Character relationships and qualities: Minli—adventurous, quick thinking, kind, generous, loyal—daughter of Ma and Ba. Ma—moans a lot. Dragon—Minli's friend

Strengths: well written—good descriptions (e.g. *the city seemed to be bubbling with people like boiling rice; the silver hair of his beard seemed to flow like a glowing waterfall*)—interesting characters and stories

Weaknesses: lots of characters and little stories inside the main story—sometimes difficult to keep track of them all

The novel's message: teaches us to be happy with what we have in life

1. In which country do Sasha's notes suggest the novel is set?

____

2. The novel belongs to which two of the genres or categories below? Tick (✓) the correct answers.

a science fiction	☐	**c** adventure	☐
b fantasy	☐	**d** historical	☐

Writing the first draft

This is the **first draft** of Sasha's **review**. Read what she has written and then answer the questions.

Where the Mountain Meets the Moon

Where the Mountain Meets the Moon was written by Grace Lin. It tells the story of a young girl called Minli. She lives in the Valley of Fruitless Mountain with her mother and father. Everyone in their village is very poor. Ma is very unhappy and moans all the time. When Ba tells Minli the story of the Old Man of the Moon who knows the answer to everything, she sets off on an epic journey to find him. She wants to change their fortune so that she, Ma and Ba will be richer and happier. On her journey Minli meets lots of interesting characters, like Dragon, the Buffalo Boy, A-Fu and Da-Fu.

I liked the novel a lot, but sometimes it was confusing. It teaches us a good lesson to be happy with what we have.

1 A good review should contain the following features. Tick (✓) the ones that Sasha has used.

- **a** an **introduction** that names the author, title and genre of the book, plus a sentence that gives a **brief overview** of the book ☐
- **b** a **series of paragraphs** that contain more **detail** and **opinions** about the plot, characters, themes and style of writing, without revealing the ending ☐
- **c** a **conclusion** that contains a **personal judgement** or **evaluation** of the book and provides a **recommendation** ☐
- **d** **noun groups** to add **interesting detail** to sentences (e.g. *a young girl called Minli*) ☐
- **e** **present-tense verbs** to tell the story and to **express opinions** ☐
- **f** **evaluative language** using a variety of **interesting adjectives** (e.g. *a* ***brilliant*** *novel*) ☐
- **g** **abstract nouns** to name **feelings** or **qualities** (e.g. *unhappiness, generosity*) ☐
- **h** **sentences** with **correct spelling** and **punctuation** ☐

2 One thing that Sasha has done well in her draft is to add detail to some of her sentences with interesting noun groups.

For example: in the first sentence she has built this group of words around the noun *story—the* ***story*** *of a young girl called Minli.*

Underline the **noun group** that is built around the noun *story* in this sentence from her draft.

When Ba tells Minli the story of the Old Man of the Moon who knows the answer to everything, she sets off on an epic journey to find him.

3 List three **adjectives** that Sasha has used in the final paragraph of her draft.

__________ __________ __________

Step-by-step improvement plan

Sasha has done some things well in her **review**, but she can improve it by adding more detail about the characters and themes. She also needs to express her opinions in a more interesting way.

Sasha is going to do some practice exercises to find ways to improve her draft. Help her complete them.

Step 1: Start with a good introduction

The **introduction** is the opening paragraph. It should provide the reader with important information about the book, such as the title, author's name and genre and briefly tell what the book is about.

Select phrases from the list below to help Sasha add the missing information to her introduction.

fantasy/adventure novel	lots of interesting characters	wonderful	a young girl
an epic journey	makes friends with a dragon	change her family's fortune	

Where the Mountain Meets the Moon is a ______________________________

______________ by ______________. It is about ______________________

______________ who goes on ______________________ to try to ____________

____.

Step 2: Use interesting adjectives to evaluate the book

Evaluative language is language that expresses opinions, judgements or points of view. Evaluative language often includes **adjectives**.

You have learnt in previous units that adjectives give information about nouns.
For example: **good** book, **great** book, **brilliant** book.

Sasha has only used two adjectives to evaluate the book in her draft—*confusing* and *good*.

Choose an adjective from the box to complete each of these sentences. Use each adjective once.

kind	stunning	creative	imaginative
interesting	beautifully written	unusual	loyal

1. Along the way she meets lots of ____________ and ____________ characters.
2. This is a ______________________ novel for children aged between 8 and 12.
3. Minli proves to be a ____________ and ____________ friend to Dragon.
4. The story is told in an ____________ and ____________ way.
5. Throughout the book there are ____________ illustrations depicting scenes from Minli's journey.

Step 3: Use abstract nouns

Abstract nouns name things like feelings and qualities, such as *unhappiness* and *wisdom*.

They can make our writing sound more formal.

Many adjectives can be turned into abstract nouns.
For example: sad → sadness

1 Turn these adjectives into abstract nouns.

a kind ______________
b creative ______________
c imaginative ______________
d generous ______________

2 Now rewrite these sentences so that the underlined adjective is an abstract noun.
For example: Minli was rewarded for being kind.

Minli was rewarded for her kindness.

a One of Minli's best qualities is that she is generous.

____

b The story shows that being greedy can lead to great unhappiness.

____

Step 4: End with a good conclusion

The **conclusion** is the final paragraph. It should contain a personal judgement of the book and a recommendation.

Although Sasha has expressed an opinion about the book in the final paragraph of her draft, she has not provided a recommendation.

Write an **evaluation** of the book and a **recommendation** that includes these words and phrases.

stories inside main story	enjoyed	descriptions
lost track of plot	beautiful	interesting characters
for 8–12-year-olds	people who like fantasy, adventure	

____

____

____

____

____

____

Writing the final draft

This is Sasha's **final draft**. Read the comments about her **review** on the left, and do the tasks on the right.

Comments

A good **introduction** *gives the book's title, name of the author, genre and a brief description of what the book is about.*

Giving a brief **outline** *of the plot without revealing the ending captures the reader's interest.*

Using a variety of **adjectives** *to give opinions about the book and its characters adds interest to the writing.*

Using **abstract nouns** *to name the characters' qualities makes the writing sound more formal.*

Looking at the **strengths and weaknesses** *of the novel provides a balanced view.*

Making **personal judgements** *and providing a* **recommendation** *helps readers decide whether or not they would like to read the book.*

Where the Mountain Meets the Moon

Where the Mountain Meets the Moon is a wonderful fantasy/adventure novel by Grace Lin. It is about a young girl who goes on an epic journey to try to change her family's fortune.

Minli lives in the Valley of Fruitless Mountain with her parents. It is a dismal place where nothing grows and everyone is poor. Ma, Minli's mother, complains so much about their poor house and lack of food that Minli decides to do something about it. Inspired by her father Ba's stories about the Old Man of the Moon who knows everything, she sets off on her epic journey to find him and ask him to change her family's fortune. Along the way she meets lots of interesting and unusual characters, like Dragon, the Buffalo Boy and A-Fu and Da-Fu.

Minli is a wonderful role model for any young girl or boy. She is intelligent and brave, and treats everyone she meets with kindness and generosity.

My favourite character, apart from Minli, is Dragon. He also wants something from the Old Man of the Moon, and accompanies Minli on her journey. He and Minli become firm friends and help each other reach their goals.

The novel is beautifully written, with lovely descriptions, like the city being described as seeming to bubble with people like boiling rice. I also enjoyed the imaginative descriptions of the places Minli visited on her journey and the characters she met.

There are lots of little stories inside the main story. I found this a bit confusing at times, as it was hard to keep track of all the characters and events. Apart from this though, I thoroughly enjoyed the novel and can definitely recommend it to 8- to 10-year-olds who love fantasy and adventure.

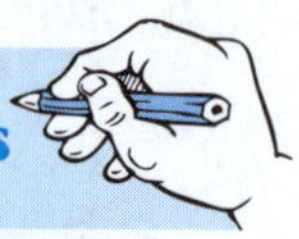

Tasks

1. **Underline** the **adjective** that expresses an opinion about the book.
2. **Underline** the **noun group** that is built around the noun *place*.
3. **Circle** the **abstract nouns** that name Minli's qualities.
4. **Underline** two **adjectives**.
5. **Circle** the **simile**.
6. **Underline** the **adverb** that shows certainty.

Student B: Niran's draft

Niran, another Year 5 student, read *Nanberry: Black Brother White* by Jackie French. These are the notes he made as he read the book.

Summary: 1789—English colonists find a young Aboriginal boy (Nanberry) with smallpox—colony's surgeon adopts him

Characters: Main—Nanberry, Surgeon White, Rachel Turner, Andrew White. Other—Maria, Governor Phillip, Big Lon, Colbee, Bennelong, Balloonderry, Thomas Moore

Character relationships and qualities: Nanberry—intelligent, caught between two cultures (Aboriginal and English) – foster brother of Andrew White

Surgeon White—a dedicated doctor, dislikes living in the colony, treats everyone respectfully

Rachel Turner—different to most of the other convicts—mother of Andrew—foster mother of Nanberry—eventually marries Thomas Moore

Strengths: based on real people and events—descriptions make the people and places come to life

Weaknesses: Some words a bit difficult

1 Which genre or category does the novel belong to? Tick (✓) the correct answer.

a fantasy ☐ **b** factual ☐ **c** historical fiction ☐

2 How much do you know about the first European settlement of Australia? Answer the questions.

a In what year did the first ships carrying convicts to Australia arrive in Sydney Harbour?

____

b Who was the first governor of New South Wales? ______________________

c Write a sentence that describes one way in which the Aboriginal way of life was different from the English way of life.

____

____

Writing the first draft

This is the **first draft** of Niran's **review**. Read it and then answer the questions.

Nanberry: Black Brother White

The author of *Nanberry: Black Brother White* is Jackie French. The novel is about early Sydney.

The novel is set in the year 1789. Some English settlers find a young Aboriginal boy, Nanberry, who is suffering from smallpox. The rest of his family has died from the disease. The settlers take the boy to the hospital, which is made up of a few rickety huts. The colony's surgeon, Surgeon White, nurses him back to health and adopts him. The novel describes Nanberry's life in early Sydney, as well as the lives of some of the other people he comes into contact with.

The novel is based on real people and events. I found it interesting because we learnt about the first European settlement of Australia last year.

The author has described the early colony very well. I admire the people who tried to make it a better place, like Rachel Turner and Thomas Moore. But I also feel sorry for the Aboriginals, because the English settlers took their land away from them.

1. Which of these features has Niran remembered to include in his draft? Tick (✓) the correct answers.

   a an **introduction** that names the author, title and genre of the book, plus a sentence that gives a **brief overview** of the book ☐

   b a series of **paragraphs** that contain more **detail** and **opinions** about the plot, characters, themes and style of writing, without revealing the ending ☐

   c a **conclusion** that contains a **personal judgement** or **evaluation** of the book and provides a **recommendation** ☐

   d **noun groups** to add **interesting detail** to sentences ☐

   e **present-tense verbs** to tell the story and express **opinions** ☐

   f **evaluative language** using a variety of **interesting adjectives** ☐

   g **abstract nouns** to name **feelings** or **qualities** ☐

   h **sentences** with **correct spelling** and **punctuation** ☐

2. Like Sasha, Niran has remembered to add detail to some of his sentences with interesting noun groups.

   Underline the **noun groups** in these sentences that are built around the underlined nouns.

   a Some English settlers find a young Aboriginal <u>boy</u> who is suffering from smallpox.

   b I found it interesting because we learnt about the first European <u>settlement</u> of Australia last year.

Step-by-step improvement plan

Niran has also done some things well in his draft but, like Sasha, he is going to do some practice exercises to turn it into a good, interesting **review**. Help him complete them.

Step 1: Start with a good introduction

Niran's **introduction** does not provide the reader with enough information about the book.

Complete the paragraph below by adding the genre of the book and a sentence that gives a bit more information about what the novel is about, such as by telling how it describes what life was like for the early settlers.

Nanberry: Black Brother White is a ____________________

____

____

Step 2: Use interesting adjectives to evaluate the book

There is a lot more that Niran can add to his **evaluation** of the book.

1. Underline the more interesting **adjective** in brackets to complete each of these sentences that Niran could use in his review.

   a I found Jackie French's descriptions of life in the early years of the colony (intriguing/interesting).

   b Jackie French has brought the people and events of that time to life with her (great/vivid) descriptions.

   c I found Jackie French's descriptions of Aboriginal customs (fascinating/excellent).

   d Jackie French's understanding of the characters and times is (good/outstanding).

   e I thoroughly enjoyed this (lovely/brilliant) novel.

2. Now write three good sentences about the book using these adjectives: *engaging, entertaining, enjoyable*.

   a ____________________

   ____

   ____

   b ____________________

   ____

   ____

   c ____________________

   ____

   ____

Step 3: Use abstract nouns

Niran needs to add some more information about the characters in his review. He has used a number of adjectives to describe them in his notes. Many of these adjectives can be turned into abstract nouns. For example: excellent → excellence.

Complete the second sentence in each of these pairs by changing the **adjective** to an **abstract noun**.

1. Nanberry was an intelligent young boy.

   From the start, Nanberry showed great ____________.

2. Nanberry was always willing to learn English ways, but never forgot his Aboriginal heritage.

   Nanberry always showed a ____________ to learn English ways, but never forgot his Aboriginal heritage.

3. Surgeon White was a dedicated doctor.

   I admire Surgeon White for his ____________ to his patients.

4. Surgeon White was respectful to everyone he met.

   Surgeon White treated everyone he met with ____________.

5. Rachel Turner was different from most of the other convicts because research shows that she really was innocent.

   The main ____________ between Rachel Turner and the other convicts is that her ____________ has been proved.

Step 4: End with a good conclusion

Like Sasha, Niran could provide a more interesting **judgement** or **evaluation** of the book in his conclusion. He also needs to include a **recommendation**.

1. Use ideas from the sentences in Steps 2 and 3 to write an interesting final **evaluation** of the book.

   ____

   ____

   ____

2. Who might enjoy reading this novel? Boys? Girls? Adults? Children? People who like historical novels? People who live in Sydney? All Australians?

   Use the answers to some of these questions to write a **recommendation** to end your review.

   ____

   ____

   ____

   ____

Writing the final draft

Niran has started writing the **final draft** of his **review**. Help him complete it, and then look in the answers section to compare what you have written with what Niran wrote.

Hint! It is essential that you look at Niran's notes and the practice exercises to complete this exercise.

Nanberry: Black Brother White

Nanberry: Black Brother White is a historical novel by Jackie French. It is set in Sydney in the early days of the colony, and gives a fascinating account of life in those times.

The novel opens in the year 1789, just after the arrival of the First Fleet. A group of English settlers finds a young Aboriginal boy, Nanberry, who is suffering from smallpox. The rest of his family has died from the disease. The settlers take the boy to the hospital, which is made up of a few rickety huts. The colony's surgeon, Surgeon White, nurses the boy back to health and adopts him. The novel goes on to describe Nanberry's life in early Sydney, as well as the lives of some of the people he comes into contact with.

The novel is based on real people and events. The characters who made the biggest impression on me were Nanberry, Surgeon White and Rachel Turner. **(Tell why the writer would have admired these three characters.)**

I found Jackie French's depiction of life in the early years of the colony intriguing. She has brought the people and events of that time to life with her vivid descriptions.

(Write a good conclusion for the review.)

....

....

....

....

....

Your turn

Write a **review** of one of the following. Use your own paper for this activity.

Writing Checklist Make sure your review contains: ✓

- an **introduction** that names the author, title and genre of the book, plus a sentence that gives a **brief overview** of the book. ☐
- a **series of paragraphs** that contain more **detail** and **opinions** about the plot, characters, themes and style of writing, without revealing the ending. ☐
- a **conclusion** that contains a **personal judgement** or **evaluation** of the book and provides a **recommendation**. ☐
- **noun groups** to add **interesting detail** to sentences. ☐
- mainly **present-tense verbs**. ☐
- **evaluative language** using a variety of **interesting adjectives**. ☐
- **abstract nouns** to name **feelings** or **qualities**. ☐
- **sentences** with **correct spelling** and **punctuation**. ☐

Tip Use **Sasha's final draft** on page 114 and **Niran's final draft** on page 119 to help you write your review.

Go to WORD BANK pages 136–137 for useful vocabulary

1. Write a review of a book you have read or are reading. Use Sasha and Niran's reviews as models.
2. Here are some other books by Jackie French that you might have read or know about: *Tom Appleby, Convict Boy; Hitler's Daughter; The Camel Who Crossed Australia.*

   Write a review of one of these books if you have read them, or read one of them and write a review of it afterwards.

   You might also want to write a review of another Jackie French book that you have read.
3. Have you read the Young Reader's Edition of *Mao's Last Dancer* by Lee Cunxin? Write a review of the book if you have read it, or read it and then write a review of it.

Answers

Unit 1 Imaginative recounts—diary entries

Page 1

1 b and d 2 b

Page 2

1 The diggers lived in canvas tents, huts made from bark and wattle and daub huts.
2 They ate mainly mutton and dampers and drank tea.
3 Children were sometimes taught by educated people in tents or under trees.

Page 3

1 b, d, and h
2 a First, Then, After breakfast, At ten o'clock, After that, Then, Then
  b After lunch/In the afternoon

Page 4

Step 1

1 b

Step 2

1 so 2 or 3 but 4 Unless/Until
5 because 6 while/when 7 when/because

Page 5

Step 3

1 excited, hopeful, optimistic
2 wonderful, fantastic, overjoyed, excited
3 despondent, dejected, downcast, unhappy
4 unhappy, annoyed, resentful, angry, furious, dissatisfied
5 angry, furious, dissatisfied, unhappy, annoyed, resentful

Step 4

1 c

Page 6

1 so 2 harsh 3 but
4 because 5 angry 6 dejected
7 exhausted

Page 7

Suggested answers:

1 The weather was very cold in winter and very hot in summer.
2 Conditions on the goldfields were unhygienic because there was rotting garbage lying everywhere and the water was often polluted.
3 Girls wore pinafores to protect their dresses.
4 Girls' clothes today are lighter, shorter and more casual than the heavy, long, conservative clothes they wore in the 1850s.

Page 8

1 b and g
2 a 4 b 5 c 1 d 3 e 2

Page 9

Step 1

1 b
2 Suggested answer:
"We're going to Australia to make our fortune!" Papa announced one morning. Although I'd never heard of Australia, it sounded very exciting!

Step 2

1 a first we had to buy a cart and horses.
  b the track was rough and bumpy.
  c Mama says we must boil it before we drink it.

Page 10

2 Suggested answers:
  a she has a decent house to live in.
  b we strike it rich.
  c some of them are quite noisy.

Step 3 Suggested answers:

1 anxious, excited, curious
2 interested, nervous, fascinated
3 confused, surprised, shocked

Step 4

1 b
2 Example: "I think I am going to be happy living in Australia."

Pages 11–12

Victoria, 14 May, 1855

The first thing Papa did in Melbourne was to buy a cart and horses. Then we set off for the goldfields! It was an uncomfortable journey because the tracks are so rough and bumpy, but we did see some interesting sights along the way. The birds in Australia are very colourful, although they can be quite noisy. There's one bird that makes a sound like somebody laughing! We also saw what looked like little grey bears in the trees. They are really cute!

I thought I would see lots of rich folk living in large houses and riding about in fine carriages, but most of the people here are very poor. They live in tents or canvas and bark huts that are packed closely together. Everybody leaves their rubbish lying around and it is very smelly. Even the water in the creek is dirty. Mama says we must boil it before we drink it, otherwise we might get sick.

Mama says she won't be happy here until she has a decent house to live in! I don't really mind living in a hut, but it is very small and cramped.

I am only allowed to go out and play with her if I have finished my chores. I like Australia because it is warmer and sunnier than England, but I miss my friends and family, especially my grandparents. Mama says that my grandparents might come to Australia when we have a proper house. That would make me very happy!

Unit 2 Descriptions—places

Page 13

1 a narrative b advertisement c poem

2 b

Page 14

1

Sight: sand, people, sunscreen, towel, ocean, children, sun, umbrellas, chairs, surfers, ship, lifeguards, sky, water, yacht, food, seagulls

Feeling/touch: sand, sunscreen, towel, ocean, sun, water, umbrellas, food

Hearing: people, children, surfers, lifeguards, water, ocean, seagulls

Smell: sunscreen, ocean, water, food

Taste: ocean, water, food, sand

2 Suggested answers:

Sight: aeroplane, shells, clouds, beach bag, hat, rocks, sunglasses, beach balls, buckets, spades, cool drinks, ice cream

Feeling/touch: shells, beach bag, hat, rocks, sunglasses, beach balls, buckets, spades

Hearing: aeroplane

Smell: seaweed

Taste: ice cream, cool drinks

Page 15

1 b, e and g

2 a is b sit, play c love d like

Page 16

Step 1

Example: There are many things I love about the beach. I love the feel of the warm sun on my back. I love the crunch of sand beneath my feet. I love to watch the waves curling and crashing onto the shore. I get to experience these things at my favourite place—the beach near my house.

Step 2

1 soft, warm 2 salty, sweet 3 cold, bare

4 happy, little 5 creamy, delicious

Page 17

Step 3

1 a that feels like sugar beneath my feet

b topped with foamy white crests

c squabbling over a chip

d of a ship on the horizon

e from nearby restaurants

Step 4

1 b

2 Suggested answer: I am sad when it is time to pack up and leave the beach, but I know it will always be there for me to enjoy.

Page 18

1 my favourite place

2 (soft)

3 white-crested

4 their tall towers, a watchful eye

5 (happy)

6 my bare legs

7 delicious smells from nearby restaurants

8 (They continue to roll onto the beach, as they always have.)

Page 19

1

Sight: tree, branches, ladder, tree house, pathway, shovel, roses, deck, grass, lawnmower, dog, kennel, father, barbecue, vegetable patch, tomatoes, lemons, caterpillars, birds, leaves

Hearing: lawnmower, dog, father, birds

Touch/feeling: tree, branches, ladder, tree house, pathway, shovel, roses, deck, grass, lawnmower, dog, kennel, father, vegetable patch, tomatoes, lemons, caterpillars, leaves

Smell: roses, grass, barbecue, tomatoes, lemons, lawnmower

Taste: barbecue, tomatoes, lemons

2 Suggested answers:

Sight: spiders, bushes, fishpond, tap, leaf blower, fence, flowers, mangoes, wheelbarrow, soil, lawnmower

Touch/feeling: spiders, bushes, fishpond, tap, leaf blower, fence, flowers, mangoes, wheelbarrow, soil

Hearing: fishpond, tap, leaf blower

Smell: bushes, fishpond, flowers, mangoes, soil

Taste: mangoes

Page 20

1 b, e and g

2 a wriggle b sit c mows d runs away

Page 21

Step 1

1 a

2 Suggested answer: I love the skateboard park near my house. I love the river where I go fishing with my dad. But nothing compares with my magical kingdom—my backyard. That is definitely my favourite place!

Step 2

Suggested answers:

Page 22

Step 3

Suggested answers:

1 the green metal shed opposite the tree
2 a large tree with spreading branches
3 fat green caterpillars that wriggle along the branches
4 lots of colourful birds with interesting calls
5 plump red tomatoes with sweet, juicy flesh
6 bright green grass on one side of the pathway
7 many bright yellow lemons on the lemon tree

Step 4

1 a = 4; b = 3; c = 1; d = 2

2 Suggested answer: I can't think of any place I'd rather be than sitting in my tree house watching over my magical kingdom—my backyard!

Noun	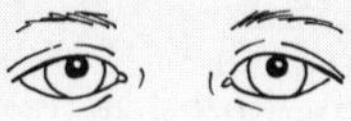		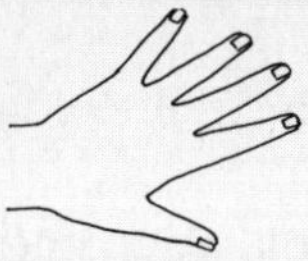		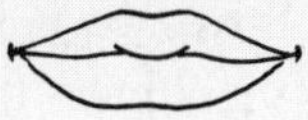
1 roses	beautiful		velvety	fragrant	
2 barbecue	smoky	sizzling	hot	mouth-watering	delicious
3 soil	brown		rough		
4 branches	spreading	scratchy	smooth	woody	
5 dog	white	loud	soft		
6 tree house	cosy		sturdy		
7 lawnmower	shiny	noisy	hard	oily	

Pages 23–24

My Favourite Place

The wooden deck is where we have our Sunday barbecues. Dad puts on his funny apron and soon the air is filled with the mouth-watering smells of steaks and sausages sizzling on the coals. Sunday lunch is my favourite meal of the week!

On one side of the pathway is a rose garden, a vegetable patch and a lemon tree. The beautiful roses with their fragrant smell and soft, velvety petals are Mum's pride and joy. Next to the rose garden is the vegetable patch. I am very proud of the tomatoes that I've grown. I love to pluck one off the vine and sink my teeth into its sweet, juicy flesh, and then feel little drops of tomato juice dribbling down my chin. The lemon tree is on the other side of the vegetable patch. It is usually full of bright yellow fruit that give off a strong, citrusy smell. The thing I like best about my backyard is my tree house. It's where I let my imagination run wild. I spend hours up there – watching fat green caterpillars wriggling along the branches and listening to the birds twittering or squawking around me. My backyard truly is a magical place!

Unit 3 Narratives

Page 25

1 and 2 Answers will vary.

3 b

Page 26

Suggested answers:

1 fierce, large, enormous, scaly, menacing
2 high, rugged, beautiful, majestic, rocky
3 frightened, terrified, unsuspecting
4 rumbling, fiery, smoky, terrifying, huge
5 red-hot, burning, bubbling, liquid
6 blazing, roaring, scorching

Page 27

1 a, c, f and j

2 a ate b went c were d was e came

Page 28

Step 1

1 a swoop b flee c flapped
d perched e gazed, spewing f gobbled
g curled

2 Suggested answers: a munched b stared

Step 2

1 a like little streams b like fireworks
c a roaring giant d Rivers of lava
e like warm syrup

Page 29

2 ribbons of fire

Step 3

1 "Oh, Flamma!" they howled, "how can you call yourself a dragon if you won't eat humans?"
2 "Oh dear," sighed Flamma, "what am I going to do?"
3 "So where have you been, Flamma? Frightening humans?" they asked.
4 "I'm so proud of you, Flamma," said his mother.
5 "Don't be frightened," said Flamma, "I'll show you all how to breathe fire."
6 "We're so sorry we were mean to you," said the dragons. "Please forgive us."

Step 4

a

Page 30

1 like little streams
2 Oh Flamma! ... How can you call yourself a dragon when you won't eat humans?
3 was perching, rumbled, rained, crawled, roast
Red-hot, good
4 rivers of bubbling lava
5 "So where have you been, Flamma? Frightening humans again?"
6 Whoosh

Page 31

Suggested answers:

1 fierce, raging, ferocious, thunderous, almighty
2 frightened, scared, terrified, appalled, horrified, panic-stricken, confused
3 happy, relieved, grateful, overjoyed, thankful

Page 32

1 c, d and f
2 c

Page 33

Step 1

1 a
2 Suggested answer: It had been an exhausting day. We'd hiked through rough bush all day, so we were relieved when, just as the sun was sinking below the horizon, we came to a shady spot next to a small creek. We quickly set up camp and after a meal of canned soup and dry crackers, we crawled into our sleeping bags. We fell asleep immediately.

Step 2

1 a bucketing b flashing c scramble
d slammed, tossing e rushing
f grasped, hauled

Page 34

2 Suggested answers:
a shouted, whispered, mumbled
b stared, gazed, glanced
c dashed, raced, rushed
d shoved, thrust, propelled

Step 3

1 b wall of water 2 c like a rag doll
3 a as thick as a blanket 4 c like a claw
5 Suggested answer: as quick as an arrow

Step 4

1 b
2 a

Page 35

Washed Away

After what seemed like hours, I stopped moving, although I could still hear the water rushing past me. I was trapped in something, but I couldn't see what it was. The thunder and lightning had stopped and the darkness was as thick as a blanket over my head. Where was I? What was I caught in? Fear gripped my chest like a claw.

Then I heard voices. "Over here!" someone shouted. "Hurry!"

Strong hands clasped my shoulders and hauled me out of the water. I learnt later that the flood had carried me three kilometres downstream to a small settlement on the banks of the creek. My rescuers were a group of locals out early to inspect the damage caused by the flood.

Unit 4 Expositions—speeches

Page 37

1 b 2 b

Page 38

1 **Supporting evidence:** clean the air, change carbon dioxide into oxygen, lungs of the earth, protect us from sun's rays, prevent sunburn

2 **Supporting evidence:** clean the air, help conserve wildlife, provide food and homes for birds, insects and small mammals

3 **Supporting evidence:** provide us with shade, release moisture into air, cool atmosphere

Page 39

1 b, e, g and i

2 believe, think

Page 40

Step 1

1 a

2 Where would you rather sit—on a bench in the blazing sun, or on the grass beneath a shady tree?

Step 2

I believe we should spend the money on more trees for the school grounds. These are my reasons.

Firstly, trees are good for our health **because** they clean the air by absorbing carbon dioxide **and** turning it into oxygen.

Secondly, trees attract birds, insects and small mammals. These animals play an important role in the environment. Birds, **for example**, help with pest control by eating unwelcome visitors such as mosquitoes.

In addition, trees protect us from the harsh rays of the sun. They **also** cool the atmosphere by releasing moisture into the air. In the hot summer months, **therefore**, more trees in the school grounds will protect us from the sun and keep us cool.

Page 41

Step 3

1 b, c and a

2 c, b and a

Step 4

1 b

2 Suggested answer: If you want to live in a beautiful, healthy environment, you have only one choice—to vote for spending the money on trees for the school grounds.

Page 42

1 This is one reason I think we should spend the $1000 on trees for the school grounds, but there are others too.

2 (Firstly), (Also), (consequently)

3 Birds, for example, help with pest control by eating unwelcome visitors such as mosquitoes.

OR

They also play a key role in pollination, which is an important part of the life cycle of plants.

4 (In addition), (therefore)

5 And you all want to live in a beautiful, healthy environment, don't you?

Page 43

1 **Supporting evidence:** have to visualise people, places and events

2 **Argument:** help us expand our vocabularies

3 **Supporting evidence:** publishers and editors check what people write—not like the internet

4 **Argument:** prevent us from becoming bored

Page 44

1 b, e and g

2 a believe b Imagine c know

Page 45

Step 1

The Year 5s have raised $1000 dollars to spend on resources for the school. The question is—what should we spend it on? I believe we should use the money to buy new books for the school library, and when I have given you my reasons, I am sure you will agree with me.

Step 2

1 for instance 2 however

3 In the first place 4 consequently

5 Furthermore 6 Finally

Page 46

Step 3

1 definitely 2 may 3 surely

4 must 5 might not 6 Perhaps

Step 4

1 a

2 Suggested answer: I am sure that my arguments have persuaded you that the money should be spent on books for the library. We all want to be more creative thinkers and writers, don't we?

Page 47

Good morning, Ms Johnson and students.

The Year 5s have raised $1000 dollars to spend on resources for the school. The question is—what should we spend it on? I believe we should use the money to buy new books for the school library, and when I have given you my reasons, I am sure you will agree with me.

Unlike movies and television programs, books don't show us what is happening—they tell us. We have to visualise the action for ourselves. This encourages us to become more creative and, therefore, better thinkers and writers.

In addition, reading books can help us expand our vocabularies. Most books are well written and often contain new words that we are not familiar with. The more we read, therefore, the more words we will know, and this will help us become more effective speakers and writers.

Finally, the information in books is usually reliable. Many people these days prefer to get their information from the internet, but anyone can write anything on a website. Editors and publishers check the information in books to make sure it is correct. If you have a project to do, wouldn't you rather get your information from a source that you know you can trust?

Unit 5 Information reports

Page 49

1 a, d and e

2 b

Page 50

1 **Appearance:** large—stiff, glossy black plumage, casque on head, bright blue face and neck, two red wattles hanging from neck, beak 10–19 cm long

Size: males 35 kg—females 50–60 kg—1.5–1.8 m tall

Diet: fruit and fungi from forest floor, insects and small animals

Breeding: May to November—female lays 3–6 eggs—male builds nest on forest floor—male incubates eggs

2 It can use its powerful kick and the sharp claw on its inner toe to defend itself.

Page 51

1 c, g and h

2 large, most fascinating, black, blue, two, red, long

Page 52

Step 1

1 Suggested answer: The southern cassowary belongs to the ratite group of birds. Ratites are large, flightless birds that include ostriches and emus.

Step 2

1 a i The southern cassowary has a distinctive appearance.

b ii The cassowary has two main weapons with which to defend itself.

2 Suggested answers:

a The cassowary is the second largest bird on earth.

b Cassowaries breed between May and November.

Page 53

Step 3

Suggested answers:

1 Two red wattles about 17–18 cm long hang from the cassowary's neck.

2 The cassowary has a brown, hornlike helmet called a casque on its head.

Step 4

1 b

2 Opinions: I think it is the most fascinating bird in Australia. I think it is unfair that the female makes the male do all the work. I think I'd like to go to a rainforest to see one.

3 Suggested answers:

a The claw on the cassowary's inner toe is up to 8 cm long.

b The cassowary can eat fruits that are toxic to other animals.

c The male builds the nest on the forest floor.

Page 54

1 ratite

2 The southern cassowary has a distinctive appearance.

3 sharp, dagger-like

4 Cassowaries are anywhere from 1.5–1.8 m tall.

5 varied, forest, small, toxic

6 Southern cassowaries breed between May and November.

7 Australia, Indonesia, New Guinea

8 hundreds, role, biodiversity

Page 55

1 **Egg stage:** female lays hundreds of eggs in slits in barks of trees—about 12 eggs per slit. Eggs hatch after many weeks.

Nymph stage: nymphs are tiny, but look like the adults—burrow into ground—live underground for 6–7 years—shed their skins regularly

Adult stage: fully grown nymphs emerge from soil—climb into trees—live for about 6 weeks on the surface

2 summer

Page 56

1 a and g

2 Suggested answers:

a The greengrocer cicada has transparent wings that are supported by veins.

b About 220 cicada species have been identified in Australia.

Page 57

Step 1

Suggested answer: It is found on every continent except Antarctica. The greengrocer cicada is just one of the 220 species of cicada that have been identified in Australia.

Step 2

1 Greengrocer cicadas live on the eastern side of Australia in cities and towns, forests and woodlands. They suck the sap from the stems of plants.

2 **Habitat:** The greengrocer cicada lives in urban areas, forests and woodlands along the eastern side of Australia between southern Queensland and Victoria and South Australia.

Feeding: Cicadas feed by inserting the long proboscis under their heads into the stem of a plant and sucking out the sap.

Page 58

Step 3

1 a antennae b nymphs c abdomens

2 Suggested answers:

a The nymphs use their forelegs to burrow into the ground.

b Cicadas produce the loud call using muscles in their abdomens. OR Greengrocer cicadas have stout green abdomens that often fade to yellow.

c There is a pair of small, bristle-like antennae on the front of the cicada's head.

Step 4

1 I think they look scary. I think that their call could harm our ears though.

2 b

3 Suggested answer: Male cicadas have organs called tymbals in their abdomens. They produce their shrill call by continually contracting and relaxing the muscles in the tymbals.

Pages 59–60

Appearance

The greengrocer cicada has a stout green body that often fades to yellow. It has two pairs of transparent wings that are supported by veins. Its wingspan is between 11 and 13 cm. On the front of its head are two prominent eyes that are set wide apart, and a pair of small, bristle-like antennae.

Feeding

Cicadas feed by inserting the long proboscis under their heads into the stem of a plant and sucking out the sap.

Communication

The intensity of the green grocer's call is above 120 decibels. The male cicadas make this shrill sound to attract females. Inside their abdomens are organs called tymbals, and they produce the noise by continually contracting and relaxing the muscles in the tymbals.

Unit 6 Procedures—video presentations

Page 61

1 b and d 2 a

Page 62

1 flaps, panel, paper, skewer, box, sheet, tape, lamp, torch, picture, character cut-out, skewer

2 remove, decorate, trim, pull out, open, cut out, tape

Page 63

1 b, g and i

2 a in the front b on the internet

c onto the craft paper d behind the box

Page 64

Step 1 Suggested answer:

Acting out scenes from the novel using a shadow puppet theatre and shadow puppets is a great way to make the characters come to life. Making a shadow puppet theatre is really easy. Just follow these simple steps.

Step 2 Suggested answers:

1 Remove the top flaps and back panel from a cardboard box.

2 Turn the box over.

3 Tape the tissue paper to the inside of the front section.

4 Decorate the box.

Page 65

Step 3

1 First/Meanwhile 2 Then/After that

3 Next/Then/After that 4 Finally

Step 4 Suggested answer:

And here it is ... your very own puppet theatre! Making it was easy and lots of fun!

Page 66

1 Acting out scenes from the novel using a shadow puppet theatre and shadow puppets is a great way to make the characters come to life.

2 First

3 turn, pull out, stands

4 Then

5 Cut, trim, tape, covers

6 on the internet

7 Finally

8 through the back of the box

Page 67

1 ginger ale, food colouring, teaspoon, tablespoon, tea bags

2 mix, sweeten

Page 68

1 b and g

2 a in 1 cup of hot water

b with 2 tablespoons of honey

c in a blender

Page 69

Step 1

Suggested answer: Would you like to be someone else? Well, it's possible with Professor Snape's polyjuice potion. Just follow these simple instructions to create your own potent potion!

Step 2

Suggested answers:

1 Pour the apple juice into a bowl.

2 Put/Place/Drop two tea bags into a cup of hot water.

3 Switch on the blender.

Page 70

Step 3

Suggested answer:

1 **First**, soak 2 tea bags in **a cup of hot water**.

2 **Next**, sweeten the tea with **2 tablespoons of honey**.

3 **Then**, pour a cup of apple juice and a cup of ginger ale into a plastic bowl.

4 Stir well.

5 **After that**, add 2 halved pineapple slices to a blender, followed by 4 tablespoons **of pineapple juice**.

6 Blend until **the mixture is smooth**.

7 **Finally**, combine all the ingredients in a large plastic bowl.

Step 4

Carefully pour your potion into a plastic bottle and store it in the fridge. Make sure you keep it out of reach of little children!

Give it to some of your friends and be prepared for a shocking sensation!

Pages 71–72

Introduction

Would you like to know what it feels like to be someone else? Well, now you can with Professor Snape's polyjuice potion. Just follow these simple instructions to create your own potent potion, and be prepared for a shocking sensation.

Method:

Start by soaking 2 green tea bags in a cup of hot water.

Then, sweeten the tea with 2 tablespoons of honey.

While the tea is brewing, pour a cup of apple juice and a cup of ginger ale into a plastic bowl.

Stir well to mix thoroughly.

Next, add 2 halved pineapple slices to a blender, followed by 4 tablespoons of pineapple juice.

Blend until the mixture is smooth.

Finally, combine all the ingredients in a large plastic jug and add 1 drop of blue food colouring.

Stir well to get an even colour.

Carefully pour your potion into a plastic bottle and store it in the fridge.

Conclusion:

This potion is dangerous! Make sure you keep it out of the reach of little children!

Unit 7 Poetry—ballads

Page 73

1 a 2 b

Page 74

1 c

2 a three b three

3 a A-cross the sto-ny ri-dges

b Comes ri-ding home a-gain

c Up Queens-land way with cat-tle

d And hob-ble-chains and camp-ware

4 And hobble-chains and camp-ware/Keep jingling to the tune.

While hobble-chains and camp-ware / Are jingling to a tune.

Page 75

1 a and f

2 a the beach b Ollie Smith

c Ollie Smith, the main character, is surfing.

Page 76

Step 1

1 a grassed, green, sloping

b soft, white, damp

c tall, young, happy/joyful, tanned

d crashing, swelling, rolling

e happy, joyful, little

Step 2

1 a strides b gazing

c curls d paddles

e floats

2 Suggested answers:

a perches, squats, lounges

b leaps, hops, springs

Page 77

Step 3

Words that rhyme with *sand*	Words that rhyme with *waves*
fanned	paves
hand	saves
stand	knaves
tanned	caves
land	raves
band	craves
planned	braves

Words that rhyme with *toes*	Words that rhyme with *song*
goes	throng
rows	along
snows	belong
lows	wrong
foes	strong
woes	gong
bows	long

Step 4

1. a Across the grassed embankment
   b Beneath his arm a longboard
   c And now he's reached the water
   d The water works its magic
   e He paddles through the breakers
2. happy

Page 78

1. sand/tanned, waves/craves
2. grassed, soft, white, Young, tall, tanned, rolling
3. And now he's reached the wa-ter/It curls a-round his toes
4. curls, banishes, paddles, hums, floats
5. right/flight, more/shore
6. To a-wait another wave / To sweep him back towards the shore

Page 79

1. The thun-der growls a war-ning
   The blue, forked light-nings gleam;
   The dro-ver turns his hor-ses
   To swim the fa-tal stream.
2. The letter *v*
3. The drover tries to cross the flooded stream, but he is pulled under the water and drowns.

Page 80

1. a, d and f
2. a in a dance studio
   b Annie Tran is practising her dance steps
   c steady, sore, tired, hurting

Page 81

Step 1

1 Young 2 sure
3 graceful, perfect, dainty, little 4 pointed
5 weary 6 sore 7 happy/joyful

Step 2

1. flits, floats, glides, spins
2. pirouetting
3. loves
4. burning, throbbing, aching

Page 82

Step 3

1. Suggested answers:
   a floor—roar, wore b well—fell, tell
   c round—sound, frowned
   d toes—flows, slows e dance—prance, stance
   f do—too/two, you
2. a sore b goes c chance

Step 4

1 Young 2 o'er 3 pirouetting
4 pointed 5 weary 6 Next
7 begin

Page 83

The Ballad of the Dancer

Young Annie Tran the dancer
Glides lightly o'er the floor.
Her steps are sure and steady
She's done them all before.
And now she's pirouetting,
Round and round she goes

Doing perfect little twirls
On the tips of pointed toes.

After practising for hours
Her legs can take no more,
And weary is her body
Her feet so very sore
But joyful is her heart
For Annie loves to dance,
It's all she'd ever do
If you gave her half the chance.

Next day she's back at training
She glides onto the floor,
Her legs no longer weary,
Her feet no longer sore.
She starts by doing warm-ups,
Then she's ready to begin,
There's a competition soon
That she'd really like to win!

Unit 8 Discussions

Page 85

1 b 2 a

Page 86

1

Advantages	Disadvantages
a fans use less electricity b good for the environment c cheaper to run, cost less d can open windows which is better for our health—more fresh air	a can't cool classrooms on hottest days b blow papers on desks away c only have two or three speeds d only help those sitting close to them

2 Suggested answer:

a good for the environment / cheaper to run

Page 87

1 b, c, h and i

2 Examples: are, use, is, cost, need, blow, find

Page 88

Step 1

Suggested answer:

I am a big fan of fans, but I also enjoy the feeling of walking into an air-conditioned classroom after running around on the playground on a hot summer's day. The question is, which is more beneficial—fans, or air conditioners?

Step 2

1

Advantages	Disadvantages
pluses	minuses
merits	problems
bonuses	downsides
positives	negatives
pros	cons
benefits	drawbacks
strengths	weaknesses
blessings	faults

Page 89

2 Suggested answers:

a benefits b drawbacks c positives/negatives

Step 3

On the one hand, fans are better for the environment because they use less electricity. They are also cheaper to run and cost less than air conditioners.

In addition/Furthermore/Also we can still get fresh air into the classrooms when we use fans because/as we can keep the windows open.

On the other hand, fans do not work well on very hot days. That's when we need air conditioners.

In addition/Furthermore/Also, fans blow papers off desks, which is something air conditioners don't do.

All in all, I think that fans are good sometimes and air conditioners are good at other times.

Step 4

While there is a strong case for using fans to cool our classrooms, I believe that we also need air conditioners. Perhaps we can use air conditioners on very hot days, and fans the rest of the time.

Page 90

1 more beneficial
2 Electricity is mainly made by burning coal, and as scientists keep warning us, this is one of the causes of global warming.
3 Secondly, fans are cheaper to run.
4 fresh, healthy
5 However
6 In addition
7 Perhaps we can use air conditioners on very hot days and fans the rest of the time.

Page 91

1

Benefits	Drawbacks
a younger ones will be safer b could help students bond with others in their year group c will stop older students from bossing younger ones	a some students have friends in other groups b students won't get to know each other c difficult to keep students apart—they don't always obey rules d more work for teachers e some areas of playground more interesting than others

2 Suggested answer: It will keep the younger students safe from the older ones.

Page 92

1 b, c

2 c

Page 93

Step 1

1 Mrs Iannella, our principal, wants to divide the playground into sections, with each year group having their own section to play in. While the idea has many advantages, it also has some drawbacks.

Step 2 Suggested answers:

1 One of the benefits of giving each group their own area to play in is that it will stop the younger ones from getting hurt.

2 While there are positives to the idea, I believe there are also negatives.

3 One of the drawbacks of separating the year groups at recess and lunch break is that some groups might get the more interesting sections to play in, which would be unfair to the other groups.

4 One of the problems for the teachers is that it will be difficult to keep track of where all the students should be.

5 A definite plus for some groups is that they will always have the best areas of the playground to play in.

Page 94

Step 3

and, as, also, In addition, A further problem

Step 4

1 c, b and a

2 For Ms Iannella's plan to work, I believe that the Kindergarten and Year 1 and 2 classes should form one group, the Year 3 and 4s another group, and the Year 5 and 6s the third group. I also think that the groups should be rotated so that each group gets to play in a different section of the playground every day. This would make it fair for everyone.

Pages 95–96

Ms Iannella, our principal, wants to divide the playground into sections, with each year group having their own section to play in at recess and lunch break. While the idea has many advantages, I also believe it has some drawbacks.

On the positive side, giving the younger students their own area to play in would stop them from getting injured by the older students. Many of the older students play rough running games. They often bump into the little ones and knock them down. Also, while playing ball games, the older students often hit the little ones by mistake. Keeping the groups apart would therefore make the playground safer for the younger children.

However, I feel that there are drawbacks to Ms Iannella's plan.

Firstly, many students are friends with students who are in a different year group but who are of a similar age. These students would no longer be able to play with each other during recess and lunch break and this could make them very unhappy.

Also, some sections of the playground are more interesting to play in than others. One section, for example, has all the equipment. It would be unfair if a group had to play in the same area every day.

Finally, making sure students stick to their area of the playground could make the job of the teachers on playground duty much harder. Some of the teachers may not even know which students belong in which year group.

Unit 9 Explanations

Page 97

1 a, c and d

2 b

3 a

Page 98

1 a stethoscope

2 by feeling your pulse

3 love

4 gold

5 c

Page 99

1 a, b, d and h

2 a Carbon dioxide is exchanged for oxygen.

b It goes back to the heart.

c It goes to all parts of the body.

Page 100

Step 1

The heart is a muscle that is located slightly to the left of the middle of the chest. It is responsible for pumping blood around the body. This process is called circulation.

Step 2

1 b and c

Page 101

2 a Waste is removed from the blood by/in the lungs.

b The oxygen is carried to all parts of the body by the blood.

Step 3

1 a left atrium b right ventricle c septum
d carbon dioxide e veins

2 Suggested answers:

Oxygen-rich blood from the lungs enters the left atrium.

The septum is a thick muscle that runs down the centre of the heart.

Blood is carried to the heart by blood vessels called veins.

Step 4

2

Page 102

1 atria, ventricles, septum
2 contracts
3 oxygen-rich, left, right
4 The flow of blood through the heart is controlled by valves that keep it moving forwards.
5 During that time the heart will have pumped blood to every cell in the body.

Page 103

1 in the mouth
2 vitamins, minerals, proteins, carbohydrates and fats
3 b
4 a

Page 104

1 a, b, d, g and h
2 a Saliva breaks down the chemicals in the food.
b They help break the food down even further.

Page 105

Step 1

1 Our bodies get the nutrients and energy they need from the food we eat.
2 The process whereby these nutrients are extracted from the food in our bodies is called digestion.

Step 2

1 The food is broken down even further by strong muscles in the wall of the stomach.
2 Any water and minerals that remain in the food are absorbed by the blood.

Page 106

Step 3

1 a the oesophagus b the small intestine
2 Suggested answers:
a The liver sends juices to the small intestine to help the body absorb nutrients.
b The large intestine is about 150 cm long.
c From the colon the waste is sent to the anus to be expelled.

Step 4

1 a What remains passes through the colon to the anus, where it is expelled.
b From the time food enters the mouth until it is expelled takes about 33 hours for a child and sometimes longer for an adult.
2 Any water and minerals that remain in the food are absorbed into the blood, and what remains passes through the colon into the anus, where it is expelled. From the time food enters the mouth until the time the waste matter is expelled takes on average 33 hours for a child, and longer for an adult.

Pages 107–108

How our bodies digest food

Digestion starts in the mouth. Saliva helps break down chemicals in the food as we chew, making it easier to swallow.

Laid out straight, the small intestine would measure almost seven metres.

In the small intestine the food is broken down even more. Juices from the liver and pancreas are sent to the small intestine to help the body digest the food and absorb nutrients.

What is left in the small intestine moves into the large intestine.

Any water and minerals that remain in the food are absorbed into the blood, and what remains passes through the colon into the anus, where it is expelled. From the time food enters the mouth until the time the waste matter is expelled takes on average 33 hours for a child, and longer for an adult.

Unit 10 Book reviews

Page 109

1 c 2 b

Page 110

1 China 2 b and c

Page 111

1 d, e and h
2 the story of the Old Man of the Moon who knows the answer to everything
3 confusing, good, happy

Page 112

Step 1

Suggested answer: *Where the Mountain Meets the Moon* is a fantasy/adventure novel by Grace Lin. It is about a young girl who goes on an epic journey to try to change her family's fortune.

Step 2

1 interesting, unusual
2 beautifully written
3 kind, loyal
4 imaginative, creative
5 stunning

Page 113

Step 3

1 a kindness b creativity
c imagination d generosity

2 a One of Minli's best qualities is her generosity.
b The story shows that greed can lead to great unhappiness.

Step 4 Suggested answer:

Sometimes all the stories inside the main story made it easy to lose track of the plot, but I enjoyed the novel because of the interesting characters and the beautiful descriptions. I would recommend this book to 8–12 year-olds who like reading fantasy/adventure.

Page 114

1 wonderful
2 a dismal place where nothing grows and everyone is poor
3 (kindness), (generosity)
4 favourite, firm
5 (bubbles with people like boiling rice)
6 definitely

Page 115

1 c

2 a 1788 b Governor Phillip
c Suggested answer: The Aboriginals got their food by hunting or gathering it from the land around them, while the English grew vegetables and fruit and raised animals to eat.

Page 116

1 b, d, e, h

2 a a young Aboriginal boy who is suffering from smallpox
b the first European settlement of Australia

Page 117

Step 1 Suggested answer:

Nanberry: Black Brother White is a historical novel by Jackie French. It is set in Sydney in the early days of the colony, and gives a fascinating account of life in those times.

Step 2

1 a intriguing b vivid c fascinating
d outstanding e brilliant

2 Suggested answers:
a I found Jackie French's style of writing very engaging.
b Although this book is based on historical events, it is written in an entertaining way.
c This is one of the most enjoyable books I've read this year.

Page 118

Step 3 Suggested answer:

1 intelligence 2 willingness 3 dedication
4 respect 5 difference, innocence

Step 4 Suggested answers:

1 This is an engaging novel with a strong historical background.
2 It should appeal to anyone who enjoys historical fiction, especially those interested in the first years of European settlement in Australia.

Pages 119–120

Nanberry: Black Brother White

The characters who made the biggest impression on me were Nanberry, Surgeon White and Rachel Hunter. I admire Nanberry for his willingness to learn English ways without forgetting his Aboriginal heritage. I also admire Surgeon White for his dedication to his patients, even though he was unhappy in the colony. I was impressed by the respect he showed everyone, including women and Aboriginals, who were not treated very well by most Englishmen in those days. I thought Rachel Hunter was unlucky to have been found guilty of a crime she didn't commit, but instead of complaining, she tried to improve herself. I was pleased that she eventually found happiness and became a respected and wealthy member of the community.

She has brought the people and events of that time to life with her vivid descriptions.

This is an engaging novel that should appeal to anyone who enjoys historical fiction, especially those interested in the first years of European settlement in Australia.

Word bank

Unit 1 Imaginative recounts—diary entries

Conjunctions to link ideas:

after	but	or	until	although
for	since	when	and	if
so	whenever	because	nor	though
while	before	once	unless	yet

Adjectives that express feelings:

angry	annoyed	cross	furious
anxious	fearful	nervous	worried
confused	baffled	bewildered	puzzled
curious	inquisitive	interested	intrigued
disappointed	dissatisfied	frustrated	saddened
disgusted	appalled	offended	outraged
enthusiastic	eager	keen	willing
exhausted	tired	weary	worn out
fascinated	enchanted	enthralled	entranced
frightened	afraid	scared	terrified
grumpy	grouchy	irritable	sullen
happy	delighted	thrilled	ecstatic
lonely	desolate	isolated	lonesome
optimistic	confident	hopeful	positive
pleased	contented	satisfied	happy
painful	agonizing	awful	unpleasant
sad	despondent	sorrowful	unhappy
surprised	astonished	amazed	astounded
upset	disturbed	dismayed	shocked

Unit 2 Descriptions—places

Adjectives that describe how people and things look:

big	huge	enormous	massive
beautiful	charming	delightful	exquisite
bright	shiny	glistening	sparkling
cosy	comfortable	snug	safe
little	small	tiny	minute
plump	fleshy	round	fat
tall	lanky	lofty	towering

Adjectives that describe how people and things sound:

quiet	hushed	muffled	faint
noisy	rowdy	deafening	ear-splitting

Adjectives that describe how people and things feel:

rough	bumpy	coarse	scaly
soft	silky	smooth	spongy
warm	hot	boiling	scorching
wet	damp	moist	soggy
cold	cool	chilly	freezing
hard	firm	solid	tough

Adjectives that describe how people and things smell:

fragrant	sweet-smelling	scented	perfumed

Adjectives that describe how people and things taste:

sweet	syrupy	honeyed	sugary
creamy	velvety	rich	luscious
crunchy	crisp	crumbly	crusty
delicious	tasty	appetizing	heavenly
hot	fiery	spicy	pungent
mouth-watering		delectable	scrumptious

Unit 3 Narratives

Descriptive verbs:

ask	beg	demand	plead
eat	gobble	munch	devour
fall	flop	plummet	plunge
fly	flit	glide	swoop
hold	clasp	clench	clutch
look (at)	gaze	glance	glare
pull	drag	haul	tug
push	nudge	prod	shove
run	race	scamper	trot
say	announce	comment	utter
see	notice	observe	spot
shake	shiver	shudder	tremble
shout	bellow	howl	yell
walk	stroll	saunter	stride

Common similes:

as **busy** as a bee
as **bouncy** as a kangaroo
as **cold** as ice
as **colourful** as a rainbow
as **dry** as dust
as **heavy** as lead
as **hot** as a furnace
as **large** as life
as **light** as a feather
as **playful** as a puppy
as **quick** as a flash
as **red** as a beetroot
to **eat** like a horse
to **fight** like cat and dog
to have a **memory** like a sieve
to have **eyes** like a hawk
to **sing** like an angel
to **sleep** like a log
to **soar** like an eagle
to **work** like a dream

Examples of metaphors:

a blanket of **snow**
a cloud of **dust**
a flood of **tears**
a fountain of **ideas**
a rainbow of **flavours**
a ribbon of **fire**
a stream of **traffic**
a veil of **mist**
a wall of **water**
tongues of **fire**

Unit 4 Expositions—speeches

Connectives to sequence information:

after that	first of all	next	finally
in conclusion	second	first	in the first place
secondly	firstly	lastly	then

Connectives to show cause and effect:

as a result, because, consequently, therefore

Connectives to show examples:

for example, for instance, in other words, such as

Modal adverbs to show uncertainty:

maybe, perhaps, possibly, probably

Modal adverbs to show certainty:

certainly, definitely, obviously, really, surely

Modal verbs to show uncertainty:

could/could not, may/may not, might/might not

Modal adverbs to show certainty:

can/cannot, must/must not, should/should not, will/will not

Unit 5 Information reports

Technical language:

This will depend on the subject you are writing about. For example:

Carpet python—reptile, scales, non-venomous
Bilby—marsupial, nocturnal, omnivore
Kookaburra—kingfisher, carnivorous, plumage

Unit 6 Procedures—video presentations

Connectives to sequence information:

after that	first of all	next	finally
in conclusion	second	first	in the first place
secondly	firstly	lastly	then

Unit 7 Poetry—ballads

Adjectives that express feelings:

angry	annoyed	cross	furious
anxious	fearful	nervous	worried
confused	baffled	bewildered	puzzled
curious	inquisitive	interested	intrigued
disappointed	dissatisfied	frustrated	saddened
enthusiastic	eager	keen	willing
exhausted	tired	weary	worn out
fascinated	enchanted	enthralled	entranced
frightened	afraid	scared	terrified
grumpy	grouchy	irritable	sullen
happy	delighted	thrilled	ecstatic
sad	despondent	sorrowful	unhappy
surprised	astonished	amazed	astounded
upset	disturbed	dismayed	shocked

Adjectives that describe how people and things look:

big	huge	enormous	massive
beautiful	charming	delightful	exquisite
bright	shiny	glistening	sparkling
cosy	comfortable	snug	
little	small	tiny	minute
plump	fleshy	round	
tall	lanky	towering	

Adjectives that describe how people and things sound:

quiet	hushed	muffled	faint
noisy	rowdy	deafening	ear-splitting

Adjectives that describe how people and things feel:

rough	bumpy	coarse	scaly
soft	silky	smooth	spongy
warm	hot	boiling	scorching
wet	damp	moist	soggy
cold	cool	chilly	freezing
hard	firm	solid	tough

Descriptive verbs:

ask	beg	demand	plead
eat	gobble	munch	devour
fall	flop	plummet	plunge
fly	flit	glide	swoop
hold	clasp	clench	clutch
look (at)	gaze	glance	glare
pull	drag	haul	tug
push	nudge	prod	shove
run	race	scamper	trot
say	announce	comment	utter
see	notice	observe	spot
shake	shiver	shudder	tremble
shout	bellow	howl	yell
walk	stroll	saunter	stride

Rhyming words:

paves	saves	knaves	caves
	raves	craves	braves
goes	rows	snows	lows
	foes	woes	bows
fanned	hand	tanned	stand
	land	band	planned
throng	along	wrong	strong
	gong	long	

Unit 8 Discussions

Connectives to show different ideas:

although, but, however, instead, nevertheless, on the other hand, whereas, yet

Connectives to sequence information:

after that	first of all	next	finally
in conclusion	second	first	in the first place
secondly	firstly	lastly	then

Connectives to show cause and effect:

as a result, because, consequently, therefore

Connectives to show examples:

for example, for instance, in other words, such as

Synonyms and antonyms:

advantages/disadvantages	benefits/drawbacks
for/against	merits/downsides
positives/negatives	pluses/minuses
pros/cons	strengths/weaknesses

Unit 9 Explanations

Technical or scientific language

This will depend on the topic you are writing about. For example:

respiratory system—oxygen, carbon dioxide, trachea
nervous system—spinal cord, neurons, synapses
skeletal system—vertebrae, bone marrow, cartilage

Unit 10 Book reviews

Adjectives that show personal qualities:

adventurous	brave	daring	fearless
clever	bright	intelligent	quick-witted
cruel	brutal	harsh	wicked
cowardly	afraid	fainthearted	fearful
friendly	amiable	kind	helpful
funny	entertaining	humorous	playful
generous	charitable	giving	unselfish
mean	greedy	nasty	selfish
neat	tidy	smart	spotless
outgoing	warm	open	friendly
shy	timid	coy	reserved
stylish	fashionable	trendy	slick

Adjectives that show opinions:

amazing	brilliant	fantastic	wonderful
bad	awful	dreadful	terrible
good	excellent	great	superb
difficult	hard	demanding	challenging
easy	simple	clear	straightforward
enjoyable	amusing	delightful	satisfying
interesting	engaging	intriguing	stimulating
strange	odd	weird	different
surprising	remarkable	unforeseen	unpredictable
unusual	incredible	memorable	unexpected

Abstract nouns that express feelings:

amazement	astonishment	awe	wonder
anger	annoyance	fury	rage
anxiety	nervousness	worry	panic
despair	gloom	despondency	dejection
embarrassment	shame	humiliation	distress
envy	jealousy	covetousness	ill will
excitement	enthusiasm	exhilaration	thrill
fear	horror	dread	terror
grief	sorrow	sadness	misery
happiness	elation	joy	bliss
hate	dislike	enmity	resentment
hope	belief	faith	optimism
love	adoration	fondness	devotion
pride	dignity	honour	self-respect
sympathy	empathy	understanding	tenderness

Abstract nouns that express qualities:

bravery	daring	fearlessness	courage
compassion	mercy	kindness	tenderness
cowardice	gutlessness	faintheartedness	fearfulness
cruelty	barbarity	savagery	brutality
curiosity	interest	inquisitiveness	nosiness
determination	boldness	persistence	steadfastness
friendliness	warmth	sociability	neighbourliness
honesty	sincerity	trustworthiness	frankness
humility	shyness	timidity	meekness
impatience	restlessness	agitation	edginess
intelligence	cleverness	brilliance	wisdom
patience	diligence	perseverance	endurance

Notes